W9-APU-575

PRACTICAL TIPS FOR
PUBLISHING SCHOLARLY ARTICLES

Also available from Lyceum Books, Inc.

Advisory Editor: Thomas M. Meenaghan, *New York University*

THE USE OF SELF: THE ESSENCE OF PROFESSIONAL EDUCATION
by Raymond Fox

CAREER REFLECTIONS OF SOCIAL WORK EDUCATORS
by Spencer Zeiger

EDUCATING FOR SOCIAL JUSTICE:
TRANSFORMATIVE EXPERIENTIAL LEARNING
edited by Julie Birkenmaier, Ashley Cruce, Jan Wilson, Jami Curley,
Ellen Burkemper, and John Stretch

CASE MANAGEMENT: AN INTRODUCTION TO
CONCEPTS AND SKILLS, THIRD EDITION
by Arthur J. Frankel and Sheldon R. Gelman

UNDERSTANDING AND MANAGING THE
THERAPEUTIC RELATIONSHIP
by Fred McKenzie

USING THE LAW: PRACTICAL DECISION MAKING IN
MENTAL HEALTH
by Andrew B. Israel

DIVERSITY IN FAMILY CONSTELLATIONS:
IMPLICATIONS FOR PRACTICE
edited by Krishna L. Guadalupe and Debra L. Welkley

CHILDREN AND LOSS: A PRACTICAL HANDBOOK
FOR PROFESSIONALS
edited by Elizabeth C. Pomeroy and Renée Bradford Garcia

ADVOCACY PRACTICE FOR SOCIAL JUSTICE, SECOND EDITION
by Richard Hoefer

THE COSTS OF COURAGE: COMBAT STRESS, WARRIORS,
AND FAMILY SURVIVAL
by Josephine G. Pryce, Colonel David H. Pryce, and
Kimberly K. Shackelford

SOCIAL WORK PRACTICE WITH LATINOS:
KEY ISSUES AND EMERGING THEMES
edited by Rich Furman and Nalini Negi

PRACTICAL TIPS FOR PUBLISHING SCHOLARLY ARTICLES
WRITING AND PUBLISHING IN THE HELPING PROFESSIONS

Second edition

Rich Furman
University of Washington Tacoma

Julie T. Kinn
*Department of Defense,
National Center for Telehealth and Technology*

LYCEUM
BOOKS, INC.

Chicago, Illinois

© 2012 by Lyceum Books, Inc.

Published by

LYCEUM BOOKS, INC.
5758 S. Blackstone Avenue
Chicago, Illinois 60637
773-643-1903 fax
773-643-1902 phone
lyceum@lyceumbooks.com
www.lyceumbooks.com

All rights reserved under International and Pan-American Copyright Conventions. No part of this publication may be reproduced, stored in a retrieval system, copied, or transmitted, in any form or by any means without written permission from the publisher.

6 5 4 3 2 1   12 13 14 15 16

ISBN 978-1-935871-10-1

Printed in the United States of America.

Library of Congress Cataloging-in-Publication Data

Furman, Rich.
   Practical tips for publishing scholarly articles : writing and publishing in the helping professions / Rich Furman, Julie T. Kinn. — 2nd ed.
      p. cm.
   Includes bibliographical references and index.
   ISBN 978-1-935871-10-1 (pbk. : alk. paper)
 I. Kinn, Julie T. II. Title.
   PN146.F87   2012
   808'.02—dc23
                                                    2011025746

To Jill
You will always be spotted to me.

To Gil Schoenstein
1964–2004
Life is good.

To Buster
1993–2005
For teaching me to be Bulldoggie.

—Rich Furman

To Jason
For teaching me how to make coffee.

—Julie Kinn

CONTENTS

Preface to the First Edition

RICH FURMAN

As are many good ideas, this book was born over food: garlic shrimp, no celery, as I recall. One week before he was to move to Washington State, Bob Jackson, a dear friend and colleague, mentioned to me that one of the key tasks of his new position would be to mentor junior faculty in the publishing process—not in research, but in publishing. A couple of years away from tenure, several faculty members in his new department were in trouble. They had not published. Some of them were fine or excellent teachers, even creative and productive researchers, but they had not published the results of their scholarship. I have known other faculty who are wonderful scholars, who conduct meaningful research and powerful program evaluations, but somehow have not disseminated their findings. What a loss to our professions that some of our colleagues' best ideas never make the journey from the mind or unpublished monograph to the published page. Bob and I lamented that while there were many valuable books on writing, and certainly excellent texts on conducting research of various kinds, none of these really teach junior faculty, graduate students, or practitioners the processes and skills needed to take an idea from conception to publication. It dawned on us that such a book could be a great resource for those who wanted or needed to publish articles in human services journals. By the time we'd finished our egg rolls, ideas were flying, and Bob had persuaded me that I should be the one to write this book.

As is true with most people who have learned to be successful in publishing, many of my lessons have come from the school of hard knocks; numerous mistakes have helped me develop the insights contained in this book. I have learned through trial and error and through a careful assessment of what has and has not worked. I also have learned by asking authors about their own publication experiences. My experience, my distillation of their ideas, and the developing of a few new techniques seem to have achieved results. In the past ten years, more than ninety of my articles have been accepted for publication in peer-reviewed journals. I do not attribute these successes to any particular brilliance. While I believe myself to be a creative and competent scholar, I am by no means an academic superstar. I do believe I am a good writer and I know that I enjoy writing, but, as I will discuss, the aptitude and enjoyment of writing can be learned. Newell (2000), editor of the journal *Clinical Effectiveness in Nursing*, agrees that success in publication is less originality of ideas and more a function of developing a set of skills (most of which you already possess) through practice. He notes that the more consistently these skills are practiced, the easier it becomes to publish.

Faculty and practitioners who have numerous publications are usually those who have their writing and publishing "muscles" stretched and conditioned; rarely are they so out of practice that they are stymied by long stretches of inactivity. While it is true that you do possess many of the skills that you need in order to publish, it is also clear that academics do not naturally or automatically learn the processes of writing for publication or submitting manuscripts. In truth, dissertations are very much anti-articles, in that they are overly repetitive, far too dense, and usually characterized by over-elaboration. Sadly, it is often erroneously assumed that graduate school training prepares us to publish our scholarship (Blaxter, Hughes, & Tight, 1998). You must carefully hone your new skills and you must learn new processes. It has been noted that artists would not expect the beginner to produce a masterpiece without guidance (Heinrich, Neese, Rogers, & Facente, 2004).

This is an important point, because beginning scholars and practitioners who want to publish too often feel inadequate and afraid to submit their work. Fear is natural and normal and can be overcome with training and effort. I hope this book will provide you with some of the guidance you need to demystify the process of publishing scholarship and that it will offer you useful tips for becoming a more effective writer of academic articles.

I believe I have achieved results in publishing articles from a careful analysis of each element in the process of publication. This book explores each of these elements. Not only have I practiced and refined these methods for myself, but I also have shared them with colleagues. Those who have used many of the ideas in this book have seen measurable results. I sincerely hope these methods also work for you. The methods espoused here are not rules written in stone: they are suggestions that you should modify to meet your own needs, given the realities of your discipline and research. If you disagree with some of the procedures advocated in this book, I hope you are able to develop new methods that work well for you. If you do develop new methods or have your own techniques that you find useful, I would love it if you would share them with me. I also hope you share these experiences with your colleagues, as too little has been written on this essential topic.

This book is not only for academics, but also for practitioners. Too many important journals in the human services fields seem to lack the wisdom and experience of practitioners. It is my hope that more practitioners develop the skills and confidence to publish their work. While this book is geared toward the human services and helping fields, broadly defined (including social work, education, nursing, counseling, psychology, public administration, criminal justice, etc.), it also may be appropriate for those in other disciplines.

Developing the ability to write for publication demands that scholars and practitioners explore their own personal and professional limitations (Murray & MacKay, 1998). Developing as an author demands that you look at your affective tendencies in addition to your cognitive and behavioral skill set. Information and exercises in this book will help you develop the confidence and emotional resources you will need for success in publishing your work.

Throughout this book you will find three tools that I use to illustrate many of the concepts and skills that I explore. First, I frequently use examples from my own scholarship and writing program. For instance, you will find article titles and abstracts, freewriting exercises, a sample submission letter and two revision letters, as well as other sample documents. These real-world examples illuminate and make real many of the issues explored throughout this guide. Second, I present the story of Dr. Karmen Lanzer in several chapters. Karmen's real-life story will help illustrate many of the points made in the book, and I hope it inspires you to begin or to continue your writing and publishing adventures. Third, I have created exercises to help you practice many different skills needed in publishing and writing. These skills will become more real to you through practice, and over time you will be able to make them your own. You can find the exercises at the end of chapters 2 through 4. Before you begin reading chapter 1, I suggest that you complete exercise 1, Introduction to Publication: Sentence Completion Exercise.

I would like to share two ideas that my mentees have insisted I include early in this text. First, you will publish. Fear not: follow the guidelines in this book, work hard, and over time you will meet your publishing goals. Second, every article has a home. Let me say that again: every article has a home. You may have to revise and submit your work many times before it will be published, but it will be published. Remember that publishing is a process, not an event; it takes time and effort, but you can do it!

PREFACE TO THE SECOND EDITION

JULIE KINN

When I read the first edition of *Practical Tips for Publishing Scholarly Articles*, I was particularly struck by two things. First, I was amazed at how much advice Rich manages to squeeze into such a small volume. Second, I was struck by the tone of the book. Rich doesn't treat writing as a lone activity occurring in the Ivory Tower. Instead, he offers us goals that all of us can accomplish. I've described it as a pep talk in book form. My hope for the second edition is that the additional topics and strategies will provide similar encouragement.

The second edition includes additional exercises to improve both your writing and your process of writing. Throughout the book you will find several vignettes written by other published authors who share their advice for successful publication. Another notable change is the increased focus on overcoming emotional impediments to writing. In particular, we provide expanded sections on stress, procrastination, and deadlines. It's likely that developing more insight into your own work process will help several of your work domains, in addition to writing.

I recommend viewing this book as a collection of potential writing tools. Give each technique consideration, try it out, and see if it works for you. Build your toolbox full of strategies to help you meet your publication goals. What works for one writer may not work for another. (For example, I am certain that "a very small snifter of single malt scotch" [chapter 3] would do nothing for my writing, but apparently it helps Rich. Perhaps we should caution you to try some of the strategies in moderation.)

To continue the pep talk theme, allow me to open with this: "Publishing is within reach!" You have something to contribute, and the world wants to read it. Visit our Facebook page (search term "Practical Tips for Publishing") to let us know your progress and what has worked for you.

ACKNOWLEDGMENTS

First, thanks to the many colleagues who taught me, usually by example, the many lessons distilled in this book. Thanks to those who have allowed me to be a part of their development and growth as scholars. For each of you to have ever called me a mentor is humbling—I have learned perhaps more from you than you have from me. Thanks to all of you, and especially Kimberly Bender, Nalini Negi, Carol Langer, and Linda Hurley Ishem. Each of you has been enormously important to my own growth and development.

Bob Jackson: Your many years of friendship have been an enormous source of support and inspiration. It was your suggestion that I write this book. A decade after we first spoke about it, here is the second edition. Cheers, Bob.

Roger Roffman: Your words of wisdom and support mean more than you will ever know. You have been priceless to me.

Jerry Finn: Your support has also been invaluable. Enjoy ping-pong in your retirement.

Beth Rushing: You were the best boss I have ever had.

Thanks to David Follmer for believing in me and in this book, and to the wonderful folks at Lyceum Books.

Of course, thanks to my family. Without your love and support, this book would never have been written. Myah and Rebecca, thank you for the gift of yourselves. Jill, you are an editor extraordinaire. Mostly, you are my heart.

—Rich Furman

Many thanks to those who have taught me collaboration, including Jim Cook, Karina Reyes, Jennifer June, and of course my favorite daily collaborator and best friend, Jason Kinn.

I also want to thank Jennifer June, Carolyn Liebler, Michael Marks, Amanda Edwards-Stewart, and Jenna Watling Neal for sharing the benefit of their experience (and for letting us publish it!).

—Julie Kinn

Exercise 1

INTRODUCTION TO PUBLICATION: SENTENCE COMPLETION EXERCISE

1. When I think of writing for publication I feel. . . .

2. Papers of publishable quality must be. . . .

3. What stops me most from writing is. . . .

4. What I most want to share with my professional community is. . . .

5. What I most want to share about my work is. . . .

6. The story I most need to tell is. . . .

7. My strengths as a writer and publishing author are. . . .

8. My limitations as a writer and publishing author are. . . .

Chapter 1

WHY WRITE AND PUBLISH?
EXPLORING AND INCREASING
MOTIVATION

There are many reasons why as an academic you may wish to work toward a systematic writing and publishing agenda. While it may seem obvious, exploring the various reasons you write—or want to write—may help improve your motivation. The more reasons that you find an activity important, the more likely you are to commit to it. Commitment can be a problem sometimes: scholars and practitioners are extremely busy people and must prioritize the use of their time after carefully considering the potential benefits.

WRITING AS A METHOD OF LEARNING AND INQUIRY

Perhaps the most important reason to write is that writing is a method of inquiry. When we want to learn about a subject, one of the most powerful ways of doing so is to write about it. Richardson (2000) conceptualizes writing as a valid method of inquiry in and of itself. When we read articles and books as we work on our scholarship, we acquire new knowledge and develop a new understanding about our topic. We simultaneously become aware of our current knowledge and gaps in our understanding. We begin to work at expanding what we know and filling in the holes of our understanding.

As we begin to write about our topic, we start to organize our thoughts and ideas into a coherent whole (Newell, 2000). For example, as we start to develop the literature review section of an article (or perhaps an entire literature review article), we move beyond the mere absorption of new knowledge and facts and into a process of creating new theories, ideas, or ways of approaching problems.

1

The process of writing forces us to compare and contrast ideas, and to deeply consider the connections among seemingly disparate facts and theories. As we move from reading to writing, we shift from a passive to an active mode of inquiry. We become creators of that which is new, ideas become related to one another in new ways, and we begin to put our stamp on the subject.

Another advantage of writing is that we begin to remember ideas, concepts, and applications that we once knew but have forgotten. When we begin to write, we must come to understand what we know, what we do not know, and what we are not sure that we know. As we write deeply and passionately about a subject, the very process of writing helps us penetrate the subject and allows us to develop new ways of perceiving it. In a very real sense, we write our way into a new relationship with the topic. The process of writing inspires our creativity and original thinking (Runco & Pritzker, 1999). Writing is a powerful process that can serve as a catalyst for creative new ideas and that helps us explore new and exciting aspects of our areas of research and practice interests. This is one of the key reasons why journaling exercises, which will be explored in more depth in other chapters, are such valuable tools.

WRITING TO IMPROVE TEACHING AND PRACTICE

The process of writing not only facilitates our exploration of a topic, but also helps us become more effective practitioners and teachers. It is often assumed that those who engage in writing and research are somehow divorced from the world of practice. This is often untrue: research is often conducted in community-based settings in which researchers develop new insights into the real-life world of practice. It is also a myth that educators are either good teachers or good scholars, but never both. As mentioned above, the act of writing helps us become clearer about our ideas and the connections among them.

Writing about a topic is one of the best ways to prepare to teach. When I (Rich) struggle with how to teach a concept, I try to do some freewriting exercises (discussed in chapter 3) as a means of sparking creativity and exploring where I am stuck. This often helps me understand why I am struggling with the concept, anticipate students' potential areas of struggle, and achieve new clarity.

For instance, I recently taught undergraduate students about the concept of empathy, which is easy to understand on a theoretical level but far more complex on a practical level. Through writing about the concept I began to think of examples of how people demonstrate empathy and of situations in which people believe that they are not understood. The act of writing helped me move from practice to theory and back to practice.

CONTRIBUTIONS TO THE PROFESSIONS

Each of us has experience, knowledge, and skills we have learned through education and practice. These same experiences, knowledge, and skills may be extremely useful to practitioners in our field and scholars from other disciplines. I (Rich) know a researcher who is fantastic at evaluating social service programs. Her evaluations are rich sources of knowledge about many variables that are relevant to the helping professions. Sadly, this outstanding researcher does not submit her findings to journals. What a shame to have this valuable knowledge available for the benefit of only the few people who will read her internal reports. Writing about what she has learned could be extremely valuable for social service programs and practitioners and could greatly affect the ways that social services are delivered.

One of the most important reasons to publish is to add to the collective wealth of our professions. To not publish the best pearls of our wisdom and research is to deprive future scholars, practitioners, and students of valuable opportunities to build on the knowledge base of our professions. Research builds on prior research. Not publishing our work inhibits the development of our professions. It impedes the march of ideas, if you will. It is impossible to know how your ideas will affect future generations of practitioners and scholars, but if you do not publish, your ideas will be lost, never used. Further, disseminating your findings (both good and bad) can help conserve community resources in a very real way. Helping others to understand interventions that did and didn't work can help other stakeholders invest time and labor wisely. While ethics is explored in more depth in another section of this book, it is an important point to consider here. Professionals have ethical obligations to disseminate their research, experience, and knowledge. For example, the Code of Ethics of the National

Association of Social Workers (NASW; 2000) recognizes that social workers are encouraged to contribute to their professional literature and to present their knowledge at conferences.

BEING PART OF A COMMUNITY

Although the actual process of writing can be a solitary act, the entire process of creating publishable articles does not have to be that way. I (Rich) use writing projects as a way to establish, deepen, and maintain my social contacts with colleagues. Many of my close friendships started as casual writing collaborations with colleagues. As much as possible, I attempt to involve others in my research and writing projects. This type of collaboration, which we discuss in more detail in chapter 7, can occur at all stages of the research or writing process. There are good reasons for collaboration in terms of the quality of the project, but, more important, each writing project affords the opportunity to connect with others.

For example, on one coauthored project I worked with a colleague who lives several states away. When we received feedback from the editor about our article, both of us were extremely busy and had little time for the extensive revisions that were needed. At that point, we decided to include a doctoral student at another university to whom I had been introduced at a conference. This student clearly had the requisite skills to make the revisions and was excited about the possibility of collaborating. Aside from having the ability, she was grateful for the opportunity to learn about the publishing process and to be included on a published article (or one that we hoped would be published). She did a wonderful job, and the article was subsequently published. Since that time, we have collaborated on several projects, including two that she initiated. Having been a part of these projects has been professionally and personally enriching to me. While generosity with one's own scholarship and mentorship should not be viewed in a quid pro quo manner, it has been my experience that when I have been generous with my work, I have received far more than I have given.

Such collaborations are win-win situations, provided that each person feels that he or she is a valued team member, is given credit for the work, and is provided opportunities for self-expression and growth. Such encounters not only meet my socioemotional needs for community, but also mean that I repeatedly have been invited to contribute to projects on the basis of my having been involved in others previously. In essence, good kindergarten and playground skills serve you well.

TENURE

The lore of many departments and schools in the helping professions contains stories of faculty who did not achieve tenure. Too often the most significant deficit in their tenure portfolio is a lack of publications. To achieve tenure at many universities, it is not enough just to be an excellent teacher. In fact, being an accomplished researcher may not be sufficient for tenure. Euben (2002) observed that, given the slow pace of Galileo's work, were he currently conducting his research even he might not receive tenure in today's publish-or-perish climate! Tenure and promotion committees and university administrators want evidence that faculty research is of a high standard and quality, that faculty peers accept it as being of worth and value. One of the most significant ways to demonstrate this worth is through publication in peer-reviewed journals (Schiele, 1991; Thyer & Myers, 2003). Faculty members' publication in peer-reviewed journals is also a way that universities can achieve status and recognition among peer institutions.

In many departments and universities, the truth is that peer-reviewed publications not only are important to tenure, but also may be the most significant factor toward achieving tenure. While this is not applicable for all institutions (and is certainly not a very romantic way to view faculty evaluation and promotion), the numbers of peer-reviewed publications, and sometimes the reputation or rankings of journals in which articles are published, are often discussed as benchmarks of achievement (Sellers, Perry, Mathiesen, & Smith, 2004). One dean of a helping profession program informed her junior faculty repeatedly that, whereas grants were nice, peer-reviewed articles were expected for tenure. She told faculty the specific number of publications that she expected from them on the basis of their different teaching loads, with small allowances made for workload variance. Another dean was clear with junior faculty that they must publish two first-authored publications each year if they hoped to "meet expectations" in their annual evaluations. Failing to meet this standard for scholarship over time would greatly reduce their chances of achieving tenure. Similarly, senior faculty were informed that they must also publish two first-authored publications each year if they hoped to maintain their current teaching loads.

Writing as a Portfolio

Writing for publication is also helpful in a purely self-serving way in that, much like an artist, your publications serve as your portfolio. Your publication portfolio documents your research and career path. Although you may have participated in cutting-edge projects, publications about the research are the tangible proof that you can provide to potential employers. Publications about your community program or unique intervention are also useful when seeking future collaborations and funding. It demonstrates that you are serious about your research or program, and also indicates that you are interested in promoting a broader change by means of sharing your experience.

The Internet helps us quickly share our portfolios. If you have permission from the publisher to post your articles on your website (see more on copyrights in chapter 6), you can add a link to the articles on your curriculum vitae. It's also nice to have electronic versions readily available on your computer to send to potential collaborators. If I (Julie) am presenting at a conference, I bring copies of related publications to share. After networking, I often follow up with an email and attached article. I've made valuable connections with a simple message such as, "It was great to meet you in DC. Here's a link to the article I mentioned."

When evaluating potential writing topics, it can be helpful to consider their place in your portfolio. Ideally, over time your portfolio will demonstrate a clear path of inquiry. Try completing this sentence: "I would like to be an expert in _____." What types of publications would such an expert have? What percentage of your current portfolio relates to this topic? On what areas do you need to focus your energy in order to reach this goal?

THE STORY OF DR. KARMEN LANZER: THE BEGINNING

In different sections of this book, you will find the story of Dr. Karmen Lanzer. Her story is presented as a case example to illustrate the actual application of various points we make. In her story, you will find hope and inspiration. This is a true story of a woman's journey as a published scholar.

Dr. Karmen Lanzer was teaching in a human services discipline at a comprehensive university in the Midwest. Like many scholars who teach in such institutions, Karmen became a professor in order to teach, not to research or write. In previous positions at smaller liberal arts colleges, she had received awards for her teaching. Students enjoyed her classes and appreciated her practice wisdom and willingness to nurture and mentor students. Karmen enjoyed her position, but she was not entirely satisfied with the city in which she lived and was worried about the growing research expectations of her current university. She realized that if she were to receive tenure there, or if she hoped to move to a similar university in a sunnier part of the country, she would have to publish.

The thought of having to publish was extremely anxiety producing for Karmen. As is the case for many scholars, Karmen's doctoral program had not prepared her to publish. Her research courses focused on quantitative methods; any discussion of writing focused on the dissertation process.

Karmen sincerely believed that she would not be able to publish scholarly work. She was not interested in research topics and methods that were more traditional, and did not believe that the world of editors and journals would be interested in her research or her teaching and practice innovations.

When Karmen first began meeting with her faculty scholarship mentor, she was practically defiant. She challenged him, "You probably can't get me to write, and you certainly won't ever help me publish!"

Chapter 2

SELF-ASSESSMENT OF
WRITING CAPACITIES
DR. LANZER BEGINS HER JOURNEY

Karmen's faculty mentor believed that she was ready for a fight. She clearly felt the need to defend herself against attack. Sensing her defensiveness, he proceeded very carefully. Instead of arguing with what he believed to be self-downing and ultimately untrue beliefs about her skills, he validated her fears and concerns. He told Karmen that he understood her feelings of concern regarding writing and publishing and that, despite any publishing successes of his, he felt the same way. He shared with her that in graduate school he learned that only certain kinds of research were valuable and he questioned his own desire to conduct such work. He confided that he also used to worry about his publication future and at times still believed that writing could be a chore. He struggled with the external expectations to produce. Relieved that her faculty mentor understood her feelings and that he was sharing his own experience instead of arguing with her, Karmen began to talk in more detail about her own fears and doubts. She also spoke about all the ideas she believed she had to share, if only she were able to write about them, and if only they were published. It became clear to her mentor that Karmen had several issues that prevented her from writing and publishing: (1) a misunderstanding about the scope and nature of publishable articles, (2) self-downing and negative beliefs about herself as a scholar, (3) a lack of knowledge about the processes of writing articles, (4) and a lack of understanding about the nature and dynamics of the peer-review and submission process.

He began challenging her self-downing thinking with the statement, "What a shame that such a brilliant and gifted scholar learned to doubt if her work was publishable. The system truly has failed us again!" By so doing, her mentor hoped to help Karmen reduce any feelings of guilt or shame. It had been his experience that doing so helps people feel less immobilized and can give them renewed energy.

SELF-ASSESSMENT OF WRITING CAPACITIES

Each of us possesses numerous strengths that we can use in the service of meeting our writing and publication goals, but each of us also has limitations. These limitations pertain to personal, psychological, structural, or environmental barriers that get in the way of your writing. It should be noted here that one of the areas not addressed in this book is basic writing skills. Appendix A provides a list of books and online resources to help you develop the actual skills of writing. If you do have some deficit in your basic writing skills, now is a good time to be honest with yourself and work to improve in this area. Journal editors and reviewers are patient with many issues; poor writing, however, is not one of them. There is no shame in having weaknesses that you need to overcome. In fact, each of us who is an educator or practitioner in the human services and helping professions has witnessed students and clients overcome many hurdles in order to meet their goals. Think about how proud you have been of these important people, and how much courage it took for them to face and transcend their deficits. Overcoming any writing deficit that you have can help you feel more competent and will lead to a sense of pride and accomplishment.

Assessing and Validating Your Strengths

Too often, scholars and practitioners consider themselves poor writers. Although we all have deficits we need to work on, you undoubtedly have many strengths that will serve you in the process. It is good to take some time to identify these strengths; by building on your strengths, you become more efficient in your work. Also, it is important to learn to feel good about yourself as a writer to get through the self-doubt and roadblocks. Growing confidence is an important aspect of the journey. Many of the journals in which we hope to publish have very low acceptance rates. We need to develop the ability to persevere

9

and feel competent in spite of rejections. In examining your strengths, look at personal attributes, environmental conditions, and potential sources of aid. We often have many resources and potential vehicles for success that we take for granted. At this point, we suggest that you complete exercise 2, Strengths Assessment, before continuing with this chapter.

We hope that you have learned many tools and skills after completing the strengths assessment. Perhaps you have developed a sense of your personal skills and have come to appreciate all the supports you do have. As you develop as a publishing author, you will develop new skills, resources, and contacts that will be valuable aids. You also, however, will want to turn your current strengths into greatness. Any current skills or resources that you identified will serve as resources that you can contribute to scholarly collaborations. Strive to consciously develop each of the skills and resources that you identified. Try to find novel ways of applying them. Share these skills with colleagues. Over time, you will be known as someone who possesses these skills and you will be sought out for them.

LIMITATIONS

In this section, you will explore potential limitations that may impede your ability to write and publish your work. We will explore psychological, environmental, and biophysical impediments that may hinder your ability to start or complete your work. New skills must be learned, but we must also unlearn "baggage" that gets in our way.

Writer's Block

The notion of writer's block is so powerful and ubiquitous that we will address it here, prior to discussing other types of limitations. Various authors have different perspectives on this phenomenon. The term itself has many different meanings and connotations. It is often discussed as if it were a psychological syndrome, with clearly identifiable symptoms: "If the term 'writer's block' represents a false, misleading category of writing problems that blurs distinctions and causes more problems than it explains, perhaps we should abandon the term altogether, and call it assorted referents by other, more precise names" (Hjortshoj, 2001, p. 8).

Bremer (1999) shares an important insight about writer's block. During a screenplay-writing course he attended as a young writer, someone asked the teacher what he did when he got writer's block. The teacher replied that there was no such thing as writer's block—there is only a failure to make a decision.

Writer's block is a social construction. It does not exist in and of itself but is a code word for many potential issues. Like other social constructs that represent complex human phenomena, the construction of writer's block can obscure the very nature of the problem and can shape behavior in and of itself. Writers who believe that they have been afflicted with this horrible syndrome can keep themselves stuck, believing that they have to wait for it to pass before they begin writing again. Often, this can be used as an excuse for what can, at times, be difficult work.

This view of writer's block does not discount the notion that there are many impediments to writing and publication. It just means that a writer cannot merely identify a specific "syndrome" and then expect to be cured of it somehow. Overcoming obstacles to writing demands a look at the many possible causes of writer's block. Like many other problems we wish to overcome, writer's block can be viewed holistically from a biopsychosocial perspective. This perspective is a valuable tool for understanding the problem, as it helps us understand the interactional nature of issues and concerns. What this means is that each of these three domains of human functioning, and the way in which they interact, can be implicated in the problem of writer's block. Fortunately, each of these domains and their interactions can also represent multiple entry points into resolving the problem.

Systems and ecological theories teach us that small changes in one realm can have significant changes in another. Tackling one or several of the impediments to your writing can lead to profound changes in your overall effectiveness.

Emotional Writing

Many of us would prefer to think that learning to write and publish is merely a process of acquiring new and improved skills. One of the underlying themes of this book is that writing and publishing articles are complex tasks; writing and publishing challenge us on many different levels. To be increasingly successful at publishing, you must develop

11

a variety of skills and maximize personal traits that are not commonly identified as important to publishing. For instance, relationship-building skills are essential to publishing; a good working relationship with a journal's editor can mean the difference between publication and non-publication (e.g., when reviewers' opinions are divided).

Psychological Impediments to Writing

Most people periodically experience depressed moods or anxiety. This is especially true when we feel overwhelmed and uncertain about our abilities. In this section, we describe the Cognitive Model and explain how it may shed light on our moods while writing. To learn more about cognitive behavioral therapy (CBT) and tools that can help in other areas of your life, read *Feeling Good* (1999) by David Burns, and *Mind Over Mood* (1995) by Dennis Greenberger and Christine Padesky. Both books are easy reads, and are grounded in empirical research.

The Cognitive Model (Beck, 1995) is the theoretical basis under-lying CBT, currently one of the most common psychotherapeutic treatments used in the United States (Norcross, 2005). The Cognitive Model and CBT are useful for treating clinically significant depression and anxiety. Effectiveness studies have found CBT to be more helpful than other forms of psychotherapy for the treatment of mood disorders (Wright, Beck, & Thase, 2008). Further, the combination of CBT and psychopharmacology has evidenced greater success than has medication alone (Melfi, Chawla, Croghan, Hanna, Kennedy, & Sredl, 1998; Parker, Roy, & Eyers, 2003). However, an understanding of the Cognitive Model and CBT techniques also can be useful for treating non-clinical levels of depression and anxiety, such as those emotional states that can make writing difficult.

The Cognitive Model holds that when we have an ambiguous experience our immediate thoughts affect our emotional reactions to the situation. For example, imagine you see an acquaintance across the road. You wave, but the acquaintance doesn't wave back. The Cognitive Model focuses on how we interpret this situation. One person may think, "She doesn't see me." However, the same person when depressed may think, "She doesn't like me and is ignoring me." Consequently, this maladaptive thought promotes further sadness. CBT and other cognitive therapies such as Rational Emotive Behavior Therapy help individuals learn more about their patterns of thinking and change these cognitions to help improve moods and decrease anxiety.

Tools from cognitive therapies can help us assess our internal blocks toward writing and publishing. The key premise is that one's thinking is the most important cause of one's behavior and emotions. Ellis (1958, 1973) contends that most human problems can be attributed to irrational beliefs that block people from achieving their goals. Practitioners are not so much concerned with the source of these beliefs as they are with methods to help people change the beliefs in order to meet their goals and move toward happiness and fulfillment.

Imagine the scholar who is attempting to write, demanding (internally) that she must write now, but imagine that she is unable to do so. She then begins to tell herself that perhaps she is not capable of doing the work or is not as smart or competent as her colleagues who produce so easily. Sound familiar? The writer then becomes discouraged by these self-downing cognitions and becomes depressed. Once depressed, the writer will avoid writing altogether, which creates more anxiety and depression as she proves to herself that she is not capable of producing and that compared to her colleagues she is worthless.

As you can easily see, these maladaptive thoughts and irrational beliefs tend to play off one another. They can logically lead to paralysis and the other insidious cognition, as in the example, that somehow writing comes more easily to others. In truth, writing is often extremely hard work. The notion that writing should or must be easy is an example of low frustration tolerance. To expect a task to be easy and then find it difficult can set you up to feel frustrated. Low tolerance frustration is also a leading cause of anxiety (Ellis, 1976), which, like depression and too much stress, makes writing very difficult.

Fortunately, these ideas not only help us understand our problems with writing and publishing, but also lend themselves well to methods for altering our irrational beliefs and changing our behaviors. Exercise 3, Self-Assessment of Irrational Writing Beliefs, which you may wish to complete at this time, is designed to help you identify the various beliefs that may interfere with your writing and publishing.

Each of us works best in different settings. Later in this chapter, we address the use of rituals to help you create a context for writing. For now, you ought to assess the environment or environments in which you work best; you may find yourself completing certain tasks in the writing and publication process best in different places. For example, I (Rich) enjoy writing with my laptop in cafés. At times, being around people helps me feel less isolated during what can be a solitary act. As I am working on this page, my daughters and two of their friends are playing with dolls about fifteen very short feet away. The noise prevents me from doing very careful work, but I am able to write in more broad strokes. I could not possibly edit my work with this much noise, but I find myself able to write freely, provided that my internal critic is turned off.

There are many types of environmental impediments. Level of noise is one important consideration. Many people assume that absolute silence is needed for writing, yet this may not be true for many people. Both of us (Rich and Julie) sometimes prefer a bit of background noise. At other times, we need a bit more quiet. Part of this depends on how the day has been and how much stress we are experiencing. Some people find that they need more quiet, and others enjoy working with people or activity around them.

Lighting is also important. Pay attention to the type of light that best meets your needs. Some people prefer to write with an intense task light, while others enjoy light that is a bit more diffuse. Regardless of your personal preference, making sure that your workspace is appropriately lit is important to the writing experience.

The place and manner in which we sit is also an important factor. Rich prefers to work in an easy chair, while Julie needs a table. Too often, however, our offices have furniture that is not tailored to our needs. If we could encourage you to make one purchase, it would be to buy a good chair ("good" according to your own personal definition). Being uncomfortable in the workspace leads to inefficiency, not to mention physical problems such as joint stress or poor posture.

At this point, to help you assess the manner in which your environment currently meets your needs, please complete exercise 4, Environmental Assessment. To help you improve your writing environment, please spend some time completing exercise 5, Creating a Good Writing Space.

When we talk about the biological domain of human behavior and functioning, we are referring to our physiological processes and needs. When our physical needs and well-being are taken care of, we perform various psychosocial tasks more efficiently. Not enough has been written about academics and practitioners in the helping professions and our abilities to take care of our bodies. It has been my experience, however, that not paying attention to one's body and its needs and rhythms can greatly affect writing ability. There are some basic commonsense issues to consider when exploring how your body can be your ally in the writing endeavor.

Writing is a sedentary act that can place great stress on several parts of the body, in particular the neck, back, and hands. When your back and neck are not comfortable or are in pain it is difficult to function well. Stretching is one of the most valuable ways to make sure that our bodies are prepared for the task of writing. You will never hear from a health-care professional that your body is too supple or too limber. On the contrary, our modern lifestyles promote bodily tension and stiffness. This is one reason why yoga, an exceptionally good exercise system for achieving balance and flexibility, has become so popular.

If you do not know how to properly stretch, find someone to help you learn. I (Rich) try to stretch at least once daily, and usually before I write. Having my body stretched and ready to write allows me to more fully concentrate on the task at hand rather than on how my body feels.

Hunger is one of the main enemies of good concentration. Hunger can result not only from eating too little, but also from eating too many unhealthful foods. Our modern diets are often out of balance, which can lead to difficult-to-handle swings in blood sugar and which can affect our mood and focus. Every body is different, and it is essential to learn what your body needs in order to function optimally. Too often, food is connected to many of our issues and does not serve its most important function well—as fuel to help us meet our dreams and goals. It is also important to drink plenty of water to achieve proper mental balance.

Sleep is an important element of self-care and essential to good productivity and quality of writing. It is difficult for us to be at our most precise and logical selves when we are tired. Although you may still be somewhat productive when fatigued, we tend to be poor judges of our own capabilities when we are tired. Pilcher and Walters (1997) tested the abilities of one group of participants on cognitive tasks after being awake for eight hours, and the abilities of another group after being awake for twenty-four hours. Of course, lack of sleep predicted poor performance. The most interesting part of the study, however, was that the sleep-deprived participants misjudged their own performance, estimating that they had in fact been much more successful than they were (Pilcher & Walters, 1997).

We encourage getting the amount of sleep that you need and taking care of your body in all aspects. However, this does not mean that we cannot write or work when we are tired. What we are about to suggest in no way advocates poor self-care. I (Rich) have found that when I am tired, my internal critic and more rational processes are not very keen. But this can be an advantage: late-night writing while one is tired is often some of the most creative. The same goes for writing when we are not able to sleep or when we wake up in the early morning. The brain functions differently in different mood states; learn which ones are conducive to each task you need to conduct in the writing process. Again, do not sacrifice your health, but use different states of awareness to your advantage. I have found that journaling and doing freewriting exercises when I am tired are very useful in stimulating new ideas.

In addition to influencing mood, stress has a direct physiological impact. Let's say that you intend to wake up at 6:00 a.m. and be out the door on your way to work by 7:00 a.m. Now, imagine that you wake up and realize you forgot to set your alarm—it is now 7:15 a.m. How do you respond physically? Most of us immediately experience a burst of energy. Whereas you might have been fatigued just a moment ago, you are now able to jump out of bed and hurry through your morning routine. You may feel as if you just had a shot of espresso, because the physiological reaction is almost identical.

When we are in a stressful state, the sympathetic branch of the nervous system is activated. This leads to an increased heart rate and blood pressure. You may feel breathless due to increased respiration, and you may notice yourself clenching your jaw due to increased muscle tension. In addition, during stressful situations more hormones such as adrenalin (epinephrine) and cortisol are released into the bloodstream. Fat and glucose are also released, giving you the sudden energy. This is all part of the body's fight-or-flight response.

Essentially, your body is preparing to fight for your life or run away. Your body is collecting resources for a fight to the death. Thinking in evolutionary terms, we have energy stores to help us survive in rare, dangerous situations. If you were actually being chased by a predator, your physical effort to escape would use up the glucose and fat released into your bloodstream. However, this ancient escape system is maladaptive, given our current sedentary lives. If you are feeling stressed while sitting at your computer, for example, you are not using up those energy stores that were just released. Further, the fight-or-flight response is most effective for short periods. However, many of our stressors are prolonged. Instead of a three-minute physical battle, you may be continuously stressed for several weeks or months by a work-related project.

Prolonged stress is harmful. It causes fatigue and decreased resistance to illness (just ask college students how many get sick immediately after finals week), and can lead to cardiovascular disease. As mentioned above, when we're stressed fat is released into the bloodstream to give the body the extra boost it needs to fight the stressor. However, too much of this fat can be deposited on the walls of the blood vessels. Ultimately, the fat deposits can block the blood supply, leading to blocked arteries, then heart attacks and strokes. Physical action, including exercise, decreases these deposits.

A key to preventing this pattern is recognizing one's vulnerability. Do you find yourself preoccupied by stressors, and letting that stress carry over into other realms of your life? In other words, when you are stressed by a project at work, do you find yourself more irritable with your friends and family? If so, you may be the typical "Type A Personality" and thus more prone to a physiological reaction from stress. Those of us who are more vulnerable to stress need to make time to exercise during the writing process, even if it's just a walk around the building once an hour. Also, it helps to channel a Type B Personality once in awhile: allow yourself some relaxation time, savor a good meal, or read a chapter from a favorite book. This provides your body with a break from the fight-or-flight response, and will help you sleep better at night, too.

Exercise 2

STRENGTHS ASSESSMENT

While completing this exercise, it is important that you not criticize your responses and that you write as freely and openly as possible. It is difficult for some of us (most of us) to look at our strengths and toot our own horns. However, it is important that you are able to carefully assess your strengths to be able to build on them. Spend at least two hours on this exercise over the course of several days. Really force yourself to look at your internal and external capacities.

1. What writing projects have you completed well? (Think both big and small, and think about aspects of the project that you did well.)

2. What skills have helped you to be successful in these projects?

3. What personal qualities helped you be successful?

4. What environmental factors helped you?

5. What do you feel like physically when you have had success with writing?

6. What other skills do you have that may help in your writing and publishing?

7. What other personal qualities do you have that may help you in your writing and publishing?

8. Who do you know who may be willing to lend assistance to you?

Exercise 3

SELF-ASSESSMENT OF
IRRATIONAL WRITING BELIEFS

Imagine yourself about to write an article: you sit down to write but are not able to do so. Imagine that you become frustrated and upset because you are unable to write as you wish. Imagine that all your fears and worries about writing and about your abilities as a writer stream into your mind. When you are in touch with these thoughts and beliefs, write them down without judging or censoring them. When you are done, put this exercise away for at least a few hours, then come back to what you wrote and ask yourself the following questions:

1. Which of the beliefs that I identified are most problematic for me (i.e., get in my way the most)?

2. What is logically wrong and irrational about these beliefs?

3. What true or rational beliefs can I use to replace my problematic beliefs?

Exercise 4

ENVIRONMENTAL ASSESSMENT

The following questions are designed to help you explore how different environmental factors contribute to or inhibit your ability to create publishable work. Some of these questions may require that you test different settings to find your ideal environment.

1. In what context do you generate your best ideas?

2. In what context do you do your best writing?

3. In what context do you do your best revising?

4. What is the best level of noise for you to work in?

5. What is the best lighting for you to work in?

6. Do you work best on a computer or by hand? (Some tasks, such as idea generation, may be more suited to one medium for you.)

7. At what time of day are you most creative?

8. At what time of day are you most productive?

9. What do you need to change in your current work environment to make it more conducive to writing?

10. What support do you need from others so that your environment is more conducive to writing?

11. What support will you ask for today to make your environment more conducive to writing?

Exercise 5

CREATING A GOOD
WRITING SPACE

To help you create a good writing space, one that is conducive to your writing, try the following visualization. First, close your eyes and focus on your breathing for a minute or two. Next, imagine yourself calm, in an indoor place that is nurturing to your creativity. Notice sights, sounds, sensations on your skin, and smells. After several minutes of this, freewrite for ten minutes about how you might create this environment, metaphorically perhaps, in your current workspace.

Chapter 3

WRITING AS A
DISCIPLINED PRACTICE

Many college professors fear and even hate writing, as do many helping and human services professionals. Practitioners complete their graduate studies in order to work with people, not to write and conduct research. Many academics seek doctoral degrees not to become researchers, but to become teachers. One of the best professors I (Rich) know believes she is cheating her students when she spends time writing for publication. All things being equal, she would rather be preparing for class or mentoring students.

Yet discomfort with writing is not merely a challenge for those with advanced degrees who need to write for their professions. Fear of and displeasure with writing is a social problem that greatly affects the abilities of many people to write and communicate effectively. Given the importance of written communication in today's postindustrial, Internet-focused economy, poor writing skills can have significant economic costs.

Overall, there has been a marked decrease in the writing abilities of students in elementary and secondary schools over the past several decades. Writing in schools is often taught as a means to an end, not as a pleasure in and of itself. Schools are often underfunded, and teachers are overwhelmed with the task of teaching poorly prepared students even the most fundamental skills. These difficulties often continue into the college years; faculty in human services disciplines struggle with how to balance the teaching of content with helping students that have inadequate writing skills.

In addition to the basic skills of writing, there are affective issues that inhibit good writing practices, as discussed previously. In grammar school, many of us (or at least those of us who periodically got into trouble) were compelled to write sentences after school as punishment.

I (Rich) can vividly recall the pain in my hands from writing fifty times, "I must not cut in line." The message in that punishment is clear: writing is not something you would choose for personal or professional fulfillment. Indeed, writing is often viewed as a task, a chore, even a punishment.

In junior high and high school, students are often taught to write essays by formula. I (Julie) remember being taught that an essay consists of five paragraphs, including a repetitive introduction and conclusion, and that each paragraph needs an initial topic sentence. These essays were no place for creativity or experimentation, so all of us ended up with similar products. Certainly, learning structure is important for students. However, the implicit lesson was that there is only one right way to write, and that way is neither creative nor fulfilling.

Perhaps the most profound experience that shapes the feelings of scholars about writing is the process of working on theses and dissertations. Writing a dissertation can be likened to a hazing. You perform your quota of painful, subservient rituals in the most banal, repetitive manner possible. Writing a dissertation is viewed as something to endure, not the opportunity to engage in a life-enhancing and potentially invigorating culmination of learning. This is a near-tragic cultural phenomenon, as dissertation writing should be viewed as a special time when you are afforded the opportunity to master knowledge and skill in an area of your choosing.

We have come to love writing—not any particular kind of writing (Rich writes poetry in addition to scholarly work and Julie writes music), but the actual process of writing. In fact, we do not draw a distinction between creative writing and other forms of writing. In a very real sense, all writing is creative writing. The traditional conceptualization of academic writing, in which the researcher merely objectively reports results, positions the writing endeavor as an afterthought, a nonessential activity. As we previously stated, writing itself is a method of inquiry (Richardson, 1993, 2000). Through the process of writing, researchers come to understand the connections among their data, constructs, and theories. The notion of the detached, distant researcher objectively writing down results denies the personality of the researcher and the important creative decisions in the writing process.

To say that writing academic research is fundamentally a creative process does not mean that it is easy or always enjoyable. As with many activities we love, there are moments of drudgery and difficulty, yet we can draw an important distinction between the notions of happiness and joy and the importance of meaning. May (1979) distinguishes between the deep joy experienced from creating a life of meaning and the fleeting experience of momentary happiness. We can find momentary happiness through consumption and passive-receptive acts, which demand little effort. Writing takes effort, though, and at times can lead to frustrations and headaches. Yet there is a profound joy to be experienced when you are able to overcome such feelings. Each time you write something, take a few moments to reflect on what you have accomplished. Let it wash over you, and give yourself the validation and praise that you deserve. Changing your perspective about the writing process and about what you are able to write will help lead to a shift in the role that writing plays in your life.

THE PRACTICE OF WRITING

In the game of publishing, consistency beats brilliance. This does not mean that brilliant ideas do not matter. Who would not love to develop an innovation in a field that would profoundly affect the lives of others? Practitioners and faculty in the human services fields want to help. We want to have impact and change the world. However, it is important that we not wait until we have a brilliant epiphany before we write. Perhaps brilliant, transformative ideas are not the only ones that should be written down (and perhaps these types of ideas only can come about in the context of writing more routine, ordinary insights). Perhaps the goal should be providing meaningful, valuable contributions to our professions. Expecting anything more may create too much pressure and lead to debilitating blocks and limitations. Besides, more than one brilliant scholar has been denied tenure for not having developed the practice of writing and so not publishing. To be successful in publishing articles, you need to develop writing as a practice or discipline.

In this sense, writing is similar to meditation. It is very hard to meditate well if you only do so once in awhile. Meditating only when you want to reduce stress may provide some benefits, yet many of the most powerful effects demand daily practice. When you meditate daily, meditation becomes integrated into the core of your life. Over time it becomes both easier and more beneficial. Having a daily meditation practice forces you to be disciplined, consistent, and focused. Over time, you experience new depths, insights, and benefits. If you miss more than a day or two, you come to feel as if something were missing, as if something were not right.

The same is true with writing. When you are out of practice, the blank sheet is daunting. However, when writing has become a central part of your life, words and ideas tend to flow—if not effortlessly, at least more smoothly. Daily or near-daily writing can even become like a meditation practice, something that takes you out of yourself, connects you to different parts of your personality, and helps you let go. When writing becomes a friend, a daily routine, it loses much of its anxiety-producing qualities. When you do not have to worry whether you will be able to produce because you already are producing on a consistent basis you are free to consider what you want to write about and who you want to become as a scholar. What we are suggesting is that we treat writing as a creative, life-inspiring practice. This clearly demands an attitude shift for many of us. It is not enough to wish this relationship into existence: it requires practice and work, including work on the psychological and emotional barriers that you identify in yourself. It also can mean learning to view writing as a vehicle for becoming more fully who you are. For some, this may be an extreme and unhelpful goal. For those of you who do not wish to see writing in this almost spiritual light, at the very least you nevertheless will need to develop a practice of writing.

Developing rituals is a valuable way to create a practice of writing. Rituals mark the end of one period or event and the beginning of another. Developing rituals around writing says, "Now I move from this past activity to writing, which is all I will do with this time." This bookmarking of time will help you view your writing time as something special, and signals that other activities can wait until you are done with your writing.

Whereas I (Rich) sometimes write in my office at the college or in cafés during the day, I do my best writing at home, late at night. I like to write in my oversized leather easy chair. It has a good large footrest and two very wide stuffed armrests. On each armrest I can place four or five articles. My laptop fits easily into my lap and my arms rest comfortably by my side. Before I sit down to work, I brew myself a cup of green tea (or even pour myself a very small snifter of single malt scotch). I sit in my chair and drink about half a cup (this would be the tea), savoring the gentle tastes and aromas. Almost ritualistically, I remind myself how lucky I am to be able to have this time to write and enjoy my tea. I remind myself that my goal is to write either one page or for one hour, and anything beyond that is pure gravy.

We strongly encourage you to develop your own writing ritual, one that helps you to see writing as an enjoyable and enriching activity. Try to incorporate objects and experiences that you enjoy into your writing.

PRODUCTION GOALS

"I am going to write an article today" is not a helpful goal. An analogous goal is weight loss: wanting to lose twenty pounds in a month may be a daunting, not to mention unrealistic, goal. It is better to focus on eating well and losing a pound a week, which is a far more healthy and feasible plan. As with weight loss, the goal of writing an article must be broken down into achievable subgoals. My (Rich's) personal writing goal is to write a minimum of one page a day, five days a week. Now, this may sound like a lofty goal, but writing a page rarely takes more than half an hour, or perhaps an hour if I am really working though some difficult material or a problem. The benefits of achieving my personal goal are enormous. For example, if you have a minimum production goal of half a page a day it translates to more than 200 pages a year, roughly equivalent to ten articles. In truth, once I sit down and write, I rarely write just one page. This is merely a goal designed to keep me on track and develop the consistency I need to achieve maximum efficiency. If I am in the mood, I often will write much more. If I am not, I meet my goal and get to feel good about myself for doing so. However, when I write on a daily basis, writing flows fairly easily, and I am able to continue without a great deal of effort. In sports, they call it being "in the zone" or "feeling locked in." It is not coincidental that the athletes who experience this sense of mastery on a regular basis are those who put in the most practice. It is the same for writing. With consistency in writing, it is much easier to access our writing "muscles."

Deadlines

Thoughtfully considering goals and timelines helps writers stick to deadlines. Allow yourself downtime, and honestly consider how much time you can devote to your writing each week. It is unfair to you to set deadlines based on what you can accomplish during your most productive workdays, those times with plenty of rest and few distractions. Don't set yourself up for failure with an unachievable goal. Instead, consider a more typical workweek. Honestly consider how much of your writing time is spent checking email and how much is truly productive. Further, it may be helpful to estimate how many hours will be needed to complete a project. If you estimate needing forty-five hours and you plan to devote five hours a week to the project, that puts your schedule out nine weeks, as long as you are not depending on feedback from anyone else. Next, check for vacations, conferences, or other interruptions during the nine weeks. Does this move your timeline out? Finally, consider the final date you expect to complete your project. Is this in line with what you initially planned?

You likely already create project goals and timelines mentally, but writing them down is advantageous because it helps you determine weaknesses in your plan, and also provides you with a working plan to edit and show to others. Project management software such as Microsoft Project can help users determine timelines for complex projects. Exercise 6, Setting Goals and Timelines, accomplishes the same goal, albeit with a less appealing interface.

It is most helpful to set small subordinate goals and deadlines for two reasons. Primarily, small tasks allow you to be more "planful." Assigning yourself the task of writing a Methods section may be overwhelming, compared to first assigning yourself writing an Overview, then the Participants subsection, Measures subsection, etc. It is easier to approach small, achievable tasks instead of focusing on the big picture. A secondary reason for setting small tasks is that it allows you a taste of success. As we will discuss in chapter 6, it is important to celebrate throughout the writing process. Although completing the Participants subsection may not call for a party, it will feel good to have completed an important task and will encourage you to continue.

After creating a timeline, you may benefit from showing it to someone else. Several graduate students I (Julie) have worked with report that a prime motivator to complete their dissertations is the fear of disappointing their advisors. For many, accountability to others helps keep us on track. After graduate school, few academics have supervisors closely monitoring their writing. A good substitute is a peer, ideally someone who is willing to read an outline now and then and who will not be afraid to call you out on any procrastination.

In addition, it is important to avoid derailment by setbacks. There will be times that you simply cannot keep to your timeline due to external factors. Allow yourself to regroup and restructure your time-line. Just as after you stray from a diet, it is important to return to the program instead of giving up entirely.

Newell (2000) says that the principle of change is as good as rest. This means that when working on scholarship it is not necessary to work sequentially, or even on one article at a time. When you feel stuck on a particular section of a paper it is a good idea to move on to another section and see if you have fresh ideas for that work. Or, if you feel stale on one article, move to another one. This principle is analogous to another important one that I (Rich) have learned from my work as a social worker: go where the energy is. That is, if I have energy for one task, it is best to use this energy to the fullest. For example, suppose you are writing the Findings section of an article. After some time, you begin to lose energy on the task and your ideas do not flow as quickly, yet from having worked on this section you find yourself thinking about several potential limitations of your data or implications for the research for your profession. Since these are the ideas occupying your attention, it is wise to honor them and work on those sections. Following this energy flow often leads to your being able to produce far more work than you would otherwise believe possible. Further, we continue to process information and engage in problem solving, even when not actively engaged in a task. By setting aside work for a time instead of pushing through, you may ultimately navigate an impasse more quickly (Smith & Blankenship, 1991).

We have heard some people express the fear that if they work in this manner, they will never finish their work, and certainly not do so on time. In fact, we have seen just the opposite in those who attempt this method. Perhaps you will not complete one initial article as quickly as you would have liked, but over time many articles begin to take shape, and ultimately you will complete them. After six months of daily writing, you will find that you have many articles close to finished (and hopefully a few already in review) and several more in various degrees of completion. For faculty on the tenure track, having this steady flow of scholarly work in different phases of completion is advantageous; while you are putting the finishing touches on next year's publications, you are starting others to be published in subsequent years. Having a scholarship pipeline takes a great deal of pressure off faculty who work in publish-or-perish environments. Knowing that you have articles that will be completed this year and that you have already begun to write articles for subsequent years allows you to concentrate on your work in the here and now without the pressure of worrying about future publications.

OVERCOMING PROCRASTINATION

Overcoming procrastination is more personal style than anything else. I usually break the work down into reasonable size chunks and then only do what I've "assigned" to myself that day. This helps me not to feel overwhelmed and to gain a sense of movement with the work. I know where it is in the process and I generally don't save it all up till the end. I plan out a timeline to help determine how much needs to be done daily and give myself little vacations from the work if I need it but always pick it back up when it is an assigned task for that day. Also, if I'm in a groove I let myself work ahead, reducing the work amount on other days or giving me more "vacation time."

Amanda Edwards-Stewart
University of Washington Tacoma
Personal correspondence

After carving out time from a busy schedule, many academic writers then have to contend with procrastination. For some, there is a virtual spring in the seat of their office chairs. You may sit down to work on a manuscript and then immediately bounce out of the seat to get a cup of coffee, speak with a colleague, or, for those working from home, do the dishes. Procrastination is especially easy with fast Internet connections that allow us to constantly check email and update social networking sites. Gaining self-control over procrastination may be a long process. Reasons for avoiding work vary by person and by task. The keys to overcoming procrastination involve understanding the underlying reason and trying a variety of techniques to determine what works best for you.

Understanding Reason

For many academics, our written products have few timelines. We may set a goal for drafts or even contract to complete a work by a specific date. However, when these dates fall too far into the future, one may become more susceptible to avoidance and procrastination. Consequently, it can be easy to let other tasks take precedence. Although publishing a peer-reviewed article may be a high priority for our long-term career success, tending to more immediate tasks is easier.

Try this quick exercise: Jot down five work tasks that are on your plate. Now rank each one according to importance, with 1 representing the most important and 5 representing the least important. Now rank each task according to due date, with 1 representing the task with the earliest due date and 5 representing the longest timeline. Let's consider your list.

If your most important task is also the task that is due the soonest, then that is clearly the task that needs your immediate effort. It's more difficult when an important task has a much later deadline or perhaps no specific deadline at all. What is your typical method of working through a list like this? If you are like many busy people, you complete the tasks according to due date instead of by importance. The danger of this approach is that highly important tasks with long deadlines can get pushed to the back of the queue several times. There will always be more tasks with short suspense deadlines. We simply cannot wait for the perfect time to begin writing.

Personal distractions can present a different kind of obstacle. Many of us carry around a mental To Do list, and we rehearse the items in the back of our minds. For example, my (Julie's) current To Do list includes writing thank-you notes, refilling a prescription, and returning a phone call to a chatty relative. I have no intention of completing these personal tasks right now, but they still distract me. Every once in awhile I have the intrusive thought, "Don't forget about that prescription!"

To help gain control over your personal distractions, please refer to exercise 7, Personal Distractions. You will list the mentally and emotionally draining distractions currently running through your mind. By writing down these distractions, you will allow yourself to fully focus on the task at hand. With the conscious knowledge that your personal tasks are recorded, you allow yourself the freedom to cease rehearsing the list. If you find this helpful in reducing anxiety and increasing your focus, try using the Personal Distractions list at other times. I find this especially helpful at the beginning of a busy workday and during long meetings. When I find my mind wandering, I often jot "PD" on my notepad and then quickly list the main perpetrators that are taking my attention. Usually, just creating this list helps increase my focus on the task at hand.

Some signs I'm procrastinating are (1) always using the excuse "I need to do X before I can work on Y," even when X is something like "sharpen pencils." (2) A sense of impending dread about a project, which might stem from a particularly daunting revision. (3) Feeling like I'm having a mental block where I just don't know what to do next, so I sit there looking at a flashing cursor for an hour.

Michael J. Marks, PhD
New Mexico State University
Personal correspondence

Just as with any maladaptive behavior, different people have different reasons for procrastinating. Developing insight into your procrastination triggers can help you avoid difficult situations. Consider someone trying to give up smoking. Typically, smokers find being around other smokers to be the most pervasive trigger for resuming smoking (Shiffman, Paty, Gnys, Kassel & Hickcox, 1996). Thus, during a stressful time, an aspiring nonsmoker would probably benefit from avoiding his or her smoking friends and locations that allow smoking. The same goes for writing: If you have a significant problem with procrastination, consider your triggers and avoid them. Set yourself up for success. Completing exercise 8, Procrastination Triggers, will help you develop insight about your potential pitfalls.

A common way we procrastinate is via the Internet. A myriad of potential procrastination opportunities are a click away. In fact, if you have your Internet browser minimized, you can even see when you have new email without leaving your computer. If your predominant way to procrastinate is by using the Internet, consider working offline. Try this experiment: for thirty minutes, unplug your high-speed Internet connection, disable your modem, or work at a coffee shop without free Wi-Fi. Do you think you could do it?

Another technique to try is scheduling downtime for yourself. Even when we have full workdays, we need breaks. When we try to work on a difficult task without stopping for several hours, we find ourselves taking breaks, whether we intend to or not. I (Julie) recently heard a coworker complain, "Before I knew it, I had wasted half an hour just looking at websites I don't even care about." It's much more satisfying to take a planned break doing something truly enjoyable. Try setting a small goal, such as "I will work on Project X for the next fifty minutes, and then I will take a break for ten minutes." When those fifty minutes are up, save your work and relax for ten minutes. Engage in those activities you usually do to procrastinate: walk around the building, text your spouse, refill your water bottle. Alternatively, save this time for something special, like reading a few pages of a good book or listening to a few minutes of a favorite podcast. There are two differences when you engage in these tasks on schedule: First, you are limiting these activities to a prescribed amount of time, instead of depending on your id to decide it's time to go back to work. Second, now you won't characterize the break as a failure. You aren't doing anything wrong—this is a normal part of work.

> My first step when I recognize that I'm procrastinating is to pick one pleasant, time-limited thing that I'd like to do instead. This means turning off the video games and email and usually going out for a thirty-minute walk (or maybe taking a thirty-minute nap). I give myself guilt-free permission to do this with the caveat that I am committed to doing real productive work for at least two hours after I have taken this (possibly necessary) break.

While I'm out on my break I have an agenda. I spend a few minutes examining the situation: What am I struggling with? a sentence? a concept? fundamental confusion about what I'm supposed to be doing as a next step? Have I organized my plan of attack wrong (i.e., am I writing the introduction first instead of writing the guts of the article first)? I spend another few minutes of break brainstorming resources that I could turn to when I get back to my task: Is there somewhere I've read about the concept that I can revisit? If I were explaining it to my mother, what would I say? In this brainstorm, I'm only interested in things that will take five minutes or less—no new trips to the library! The rest of my break is really a break. I look at the colors and shapes in the world around me, feel the weather, notice which muscles in my body are aching, awaken to the fact that I'm hungry or thirsty, etc.

Carolyn Liebler, PhD
University of Minnesota
Personal correspondence

WRITING IS NOT REWRITING

It has been said that writing is rewriting. This notion hinders the writer's ability to write more than anything else. According to this view of writing, each sentence must be carefully reworked over and over for it to be "writing." This is not writing—it is revising. As you will come to understand, writing and revising are two different activities and may even involve different parts of the brain. Of course, before you submit anything for publication, it will need to be revised; some authors produce as many as three to five drafts at this stage. Once this is done, do a final spellcheck. And remember that when your manuscript is accepted for publication, it will be reviewed and edited by a copy editor, who will make additional modifications to your work. However, at this point in the writing process you do not need to worry about these issues. What is important is generating ideas and getting them down on paper.

Jack Kerouac has said that he wrote all of *On the Road* in three intense weeks of freewheeling writing. When he had finished writing the last word, his book (a 120-foot-long scroll spooling from his typewriter) was finished. The bones of one of the truly great American novels had been set down in one intense session. We are not suggesting that you can produce scholarship in the same manner. However, what Kerouac and the other beat writers of his generation knew was that we have an internal wisdom that goes beyond the plodding pace of logical thinking. When set free to just write, our minds and fingers surprise us. We know more than we think we know and we are able to communicate more than we may have anticipated.

What would it be like if you allowed yourself to start with some idea and let yourself just write? What if you were to sit down and write about some of your practice or teaching experiences and just allow the writing to flow? In all likelihood, after some time you will have written some ideas or experiences that are valuable to others. Your subjective experience matters. Your training, experience, and intellectual currency can lead to helpful and publishable work if you develop trust in your subjectivity and practice of writing. What variables we choose to research and what findings we focus on have a great deal to do with our own beliefs and values. We are suggesting that you learn to value your subjective experiences as a means of freeing yourself to write.

Much has been written about the processes of freeing the mind to write. We now explore several techniques that we have found to be helpful.

STREAM OF CONSCIOUSNESS OR FREEWRITING

Freewriting is a valuable writing tool that serves several key purposes. First, it is a great warm-up exercise for getting the mind ready to write. Second, through the process of freewriting, we tend to access information that we never knew we had. Third, freewriting seems to help us get around our internal critic, that voice that judges what we write. Finally, by engaging in freewriting we come to learn that we can indeed write on demand.

Freewriting can be either prompted or unprompted. During unprompted freewriting, you begin to write whatever is on your mind for a set amount of time, usually three to ten minutes. It is imperative that you censor nothing and that the writing does not stop until the designated time. If you get stuck, simply write the last word over and over or write any nonsense that may find its way onto the page. During prompted freewriting, you follow the same procedures, but the difference is that a word or topic becomes the focus of the exercise. Therefore, freewriting may start off with a simple word or phrase such as "children" or "the causes of childhood poverty." For several examples of freewriting exercises, see exercise 9, Freewriting Exercises. Now is a good time to complete one of those freewriting exercises to help you develop this new tool.

THE ACADEMIC NOTEBOOK

Many authors have noted the value of keeping a journal to their development as scholars. Henson (2005) observes that even though much of his work is traditional survey research, some of the most important ideas happen at random and unforeseen times. Having a notebook available at all times allows scholars to capture insights that otherwise would be lost. Many ideas for articles or insights into the research endeavor come to me (Rich) at random times. Having a notebook with me allows me not only to capture these ideas before they are lost, but also to spend less overall time on my work. Spending a few minutes writing in my academic journal when my mind is most attuned to a particular idea or problem often saves me hours of laborious thinking. Academic notebooks can be used not only for spontaneous insights, but also in a playful manner to develop creative insights.

The first step in developing an academic notebook is to buy a writing journal. We suggest not merely recycling an old notebook or buying an inexpensive spiral notebook. It is easier to write in a book that feels good and has meaning rather than in a random, inexpensive notebook. By giving your journal a prominent place in your life you will create a space for writing to become important. Also, since you will carry your journal around with you, you may want one that does not make you look like a high school student or a starving artist (though there is nothing wrong with either). Choose a journal that feels good in your hands. Pay attention to the fabric and size. Some people like larger leather-bound journals, while others like smaller more intimate notebooks that fit into the back pocket of a pair of pants. The idea is to create a journal that will become a part of your life.

With a journal you can develop a consistent flow of ideas around your work, scholarship, and insights. For at least a few minutes of your day, write in your journal. You might want to ask yourself what you are curious about right now, what questions need to be answered in your profession, what gaps there are in your knowledge, what has been bothering you lately. Some of these questions may help trigger your thoughts. Your notebook is not the place to evaluate and critique your ideas; that comes later in the process. For now, the goal is to allow yourself to jot down ideas and make connections among them. Think as outlandishly as you like. Pretend you are from another planet and are just trying to understand Earth. Imagine yourself to be a curious child who does not evaluate thoughts but merely has them. Let yourself develop a sense of play and creativity.

MIND MAPPING

Mind mapping, often referred to as concept mapping, is a means of representing potential and actual knowledge in visual forms. The theory behind mind mapping is that the development and creation of ideas and concepts on a high level of abstraction is far too complex a task for a word processor. The actual process of writing on a computer limits the creative capacities of thinking to a relatively linear process. The brain is a powerful machine with billions of neural connections; the mind is able to think in complex nonlinear patterns. In other words, mind mapping seeks to free the mind of limiting constraints imposed by overly simplistic linear tools.

In mind mapping, you draw and connect circles or nodes with lines that demonstrate the connections among various ideas and bits of knowledge. Mind maps are a valuable means of generating ideas, designing intricate models, communicating complex ideas, or helping to understand information in new ways (Lanzig, 1997).

Creating mind maps is also a valuable tool at various stages in the writing process. They can be used at the beginning of the writing process to help generate ideas, sources of knowledge, or novel ways of understanding a problem. According to Doyle, Coggin, and Lanning (2004), mind mapping "can help the author establish a central focus of purpose statement, identify concepts and arguments of primary importance, explore cause-effect relationships between constructs, and use the resolving visual as a guide for organizing and writing the manuscript" (p. 107).

Mind mapping can be done by hand or with the help of various software programs. Exercise 10, Mind-Mapping Exercises, presents two examples of mind-mapping exercises that are useful in exploring potential sources for data and in generating ideas for writing and research.

Effective Paraphrasing

A common difficulty of graduate students and others working to improve their academic writing is paraphrasing. During a writing workshop I (Julie) once led, 62 percent (twenty-three out of thirty-seven) of the graduate students anonymously indicated that they had accidentally plagiarized in the past, in part due to difficulty paraphrasing others' work. Paraphrasing can be difficult if the passage one wants to refer to is complex. Successful paraphrasing is a writing skill we are expected to master, but few of us are explicitly taught. When we see that a student has reworded instead of paraphrased a passage, we know that he or she doesn't actually understand the original text.

When helping students in classes and writing workshops learn to appropriately paraphrase, I (Julie) have them concentrate on distilling the message, rather than rewording it. I hand out children's storybooks, and ask each participant to read one, put it away, and then paraphrase the book in only one sentence without looking at the book. This is a fun exercise; it is always amusing to hear summaries such as, "A humanoid character is grudgingly convinced to try a meal of green eggs and ham," or, "A young rabbit says 'good night' to several objects in his room."

After paraphrasing the children's storybooks, we practice this task with one section of a research article. When participants have difficulty paraphrasing without looking at the article, they reread the section and then explain it in a way that anyone would understand. Writing doesn't need to sound academic and publishable in a first draft. It is far more important to gain a thorough understanding of the material than it is to sound academic. If you understand the material, you can write about it in your own words. Try it yourself in exercise 11, Effective Paraphrasing.

Exercise 6

SETTING GOALS AND TIMELINES

Step 1: List the major benchmarks toward achieving your writing goal. For example, if your goal is to submit a literature review to a peer-reviewed journal, your major benchmarks could include
> pick a journal,
> conduct a comprehensive literature review,
> write a manuscript, and
> submit the manuscript to the journal.

Step 2: For each of the major benchmarks, outline every task involved. For example, under comprehensive literature review, you may list these tasks:
> Conduct initial search for relevant literature.
> Read articles.
> Summarize articles.
> Note ideas for subsequent literature searches.
> Conduct subsequent literature search for search terms X, Y, Z.
> Read articles.
> Summarize articles.

Step 3: Assign estimated time necessary to complete each item. Think realistically. Some items may take two hours (e.g., to format the reference list), and some may take several days or weeks. Add all the time required to complete each step to estimate your completion date.

Step 4: Review your goals and timeline. Is your completion date reasonable? Can you foresee any roadblocks (e.g., collaborators' vacations, other priority projects)?

Step 5: Edit your timeline. This is not a one-time task; you will benefit from revisiting your timeline and editing it as necessary.

Exercise 7

PERSONAL DISTRACTIONS

Writing a list of distractions can help increase focus on the task at hand. For some, simply knowing that the personal tasks are written down can decrease their intrusion on concentration. Try creating this list immediately before writing. If you later find yourself thinking, "I need to remember to . . . ," just add the distracting task to the list.

Distraction: In the first column, enter a list of all the tasks and other intrusions on your concentration. These may include work tasks, personal errands, and other important or even insignificant responsibilities that are weighing on you. If an interpersonal issue is on your mind such as an argument with a friend, go ahead and jot that down, too. The idea is to release all of these distractions from your immediate attention.

Plan: Jot down a few words to describe when and how you will address the distraction. Some distractions may need to be listed as "ongoing."

Distraction	Plan

Exercise 8

PROCRASTINATION TRIGGERS

Think back to a recent time that you found yourself procrastinating.

Questions about the Task

What project were you supposed to be working on?

How did you feel about that project?

Was the task easy or difficult? Clear or unclear?

Under what conditions were you working (with whom, where, what time of day)?

How much time do you estimate the task would have taken if you had completed it without procrastinating?

Questions about your Procrastination

How much time did you spend procrastinating?

What activities did you do to procrastinate?

Was this experience typical for you?

Thinking back on your responses, list your potential triggers for procrastination. How should this change the way you work?

Exercise 9

FREEWRITING EXERCISES

1. As a warm-up, on a blank piece of paper write the sentence, "Today I feel . . . ," then write for five minutes without thinking or censoring yourself. Often, writing from our own experience helps free us to write more easily.
2. It is difficult for some people to write about themselves. As an alternative warm-up, write for five minutes on this sentence: "If I could write about anything today, it would be. . . ."
3. On a blank piece of paper, write the one word that best describes your main research interests (e.g., "adolescents"). Starting with this word, freewrite for five minutes.
4. Complete the exercise described in suggestion 3, but with a concept that intrigues you.
5. Write on a piece of paper the following sentence: "Two important concepts that I am trying to connect are _____ and _____." Write for five minutes.

Exercise 10

MIND-MAPPING EXERCISES

For these exercises, you will need a piece of white or light-colored poster board or four taped-together sheets of standard white computer paper. Spend a couple of minutes clearing your mind. Conduct each exercise when you have no interruptions and can spend at least a half hour on each.

1. In the middle of the page, draw a circle and in it write the word that best describes your main scholarly area. Draw ten other circles surrounding your original word, at least six inches away. In each circle, fill in a related concept. From each of these concepts, draw three circles and connecting lines that lead to another group of circles. Fill in each of those circles with new connecting concepts. Next, draw lines between each concept that relates to another. Along each line, describe how the concepts are connected. This exercise is a valuable way to understand how different concepts in our work are related.

2. In the middle of another page, draw a circle and write the same word in the middle. Again, draw ten circles surrounding the word, connected by lines. In each circle, write the name of a potential title to a new article about this topic. From each of those circles, draw lines out to new circles that explore what the article will look like, what data you need, what skills and resources you need, and where it might be published. This exercise helps you brainstorm potential article ideas.

Exercise 11

EFFECTIVE PARAPHRASING

The goal of this exercise is to help you gain confidence in your paraphrasing skills.

Step 1: Visit the farcical news website The Onion, http://www.theonion.com/. Pick one article; print it out if you prefer to work on "hard copy."

Step 2: Read the article. Now, without looking at the article, summarize what you read in only one to two sentences.

Step 3: Now that you have practiced paraphrasing something silly, try this exercise with an academic article. Pick an article from your discipline.

Step 4: Read the first section of the article, and, again without looking at the article, summarize what you read in only one to two sentences. If you have difficulty, reread the section until you better understand what you read and then try to paraphrase the section again. Repeat this for every section of the article.

Step 5: Review your work. You now have several sentences written in your own words that paraphrase what you have read. For some writers, completing this process helps achieve better understanding of the literature, and saves time in the long run.

Chapter 4

TYPES OF
SCHOLARLY PUBLICATIONS

Think back to your graduate education, if this is not too painful. Try to recall a journal article that affected your educational experience. Can you think of one? If not, do not be alarmed: many of us cannot. If you can recall one, most likely it was not an empirical, research-based article. In all likelihood, it was something more philosophical that touched some part of you that "traditional" research may not reach. It may have inspired you through some particularly creative insight or may have imparted to you valuable practice wisdom. In all likelihood, it inspired the same part of you that chose your profession in the first place. In other words, its emotional currency touched you at the time and may still touch you today. I (Rich) remember an article by the late Howard Goldstein (1990) that discussed the relationships among theory, practice wisdom, and research in social work education and practice. The article contained no empirical data; it was based on Goldstein's practice experience, contextualized through his reading of the history of the profession. In the article, he traced historical trends and influences on the social work profession. Goldstein presented his assessment of the current direction of the profession and of how this direction was circumventing the historical values of social work. I remember the feeling of excitement when I read the article: it was as if someone had opened up my head, taken out the best of my own thinking, organized it into a coherent whole, and added layer upon layer of insights from a lifetime of professional experiences. Since that day, Goldstein's work has been essential to my development as a social worker and social work educator. It has provided me with a vision and has challenged me to continually focus on the humanistic aspects of my profession.

Articles such as Goldstein's, however, are not what most of us were trained to write in graduate school. We often learn that writing is a means to an end, and that end is to publish empirical research. In fact, one of the most significant impediments to writing and publication is that most scholars and practitioners have limited views of what may be of value, and certainly of what is considered publishable scholarship. Many of us learn from our dissertation committees that scholarship must be quantitative—or qualitative—research. We learn that becoming a scholar means collecting and analyzing data and then presenting findings. This model holds enormous value, but it is not the only model. In many disciplines, scholars are taught to see scholarship solely in terms of empirical research. However, there are many valuable ways to know, learn, and teach. This is not to denigrate research approaches that are more traditional—it is merely to expand horizons.

It is important for new scholars to understand that there are many types of articles published in scholarly journals. A great many articles in peer-reviewed journals are not based on quantitative or qualitative research methods. A strange schism exists between what is frequently published in peer-reviewed journals and what is taught in graduate school. We do not mean to disparage empirical research. The point is that different constituents have a variety of needs for diverse types of knowledge. Practitioners often need hands-on practice wisdom from those who have come before. Empirical researchers need theoretical formulations in order to integrate their work; many empirical studies are designed to test theoretical formulations. There is room for all our ways of working, and each of us can probably stand to step outside our comfortable little boxes and try some new ways of working.

Again, it is important to know that there are many different kinds of articles found in peer-reviewed journals. In this chapter, we help expand your horizons about what is publishable. Remember, it is important to understand what your institution expects in terms of publications. If peer review is the most important criterion, then you may have the go-ahead to write and publish many types of work.

When attempting to ascertain the type of article you wish to write, it is important to note that, as an author, you may have many potential objectives. An article may be designed to create new knowledge about an important topic or to posit new ways of applying existing knowledge. It may seek to explore, or it may seek to confirm. An article may present real-world applications of previously conducted research or explore values and ethical dilemmas of professional situations. Think in terms of titles and abstracts. As the following examples illustrate, authors are only limited by the creativity and insight they bring to the scholarly endeavor. In the margins of this book, or perhaps in your academic notebook or journal, jot down ideas that are stimulated by your reading. See if you can come up with titles or perhaps abstracts of your own.

The following is a brief discussion of several types of articles, along with some sample abstracts. Reading abstracts is a wonderful way of grasping the scope of your possibilities. Also, please complete exercise 12, Wandering Through the Stacks, and exercise 13, Writing Two Abstracts, to help you generate some ideas for the types of articles that you can write.

QUALITATIVE STUDIES

Qualitative studies follow a variety of formats that depend on the researchers' theoretical orientations and disciplinary affiliations. Qualitative studies often follow the traditional architecture of a research article (abstract, introduction, literature review, methodology, data, discussion, implications and limitations, and conclusion). Many authors who try to publish qualitative research do not spend sufficient time discussing their methods or the philosophical origins of their methods. We highly recommend that you pay careful attention to developing the methodology sections of your qualitative studies and use substantial literature to justify your methodological choices.

Sample Abstract

Social policy shapes the infrastructure wherein social work is practiced. But what happens when a particular social policy is seemingly incongruent with the social work code of ethics? How do social work students conceive and resolve potential practice dilemmas that may arise as a consequence? This study explores potential practice dilemmas as a result of Proposition 200, an Arizona immigration law that would require social workers employed in the public sector to deny services to undocumented clients. The six-step analysis found that students recognized various practice dilemmas that the policy would present and conflicts between the policy and social work ethics. Students also identified numerous strategies for resolving the above-mentioned dilemmas. (Furman, Langer, Sanchez, & Negi, 2007)

CASE STUDIES

Case studies use examples to demonstrate a point or to present examples of representative phenomena in an in-depth manner. Case studies may demonstrate the processes of interventions and techniques or the manner in which interventions or programs affect others. Case studies are also wonderful tools for helping readers apply key principles that you present. Some case study articles pose questions to help stimulate in readers the ability to integrate key ideas with their own practice.

Writing case studies is a good publishing option for scholars with practice experience. They are valid and valuable ways of communicating your expertise. Practitioners value case studies perhaps more than academics do. They are, therefore, good for professional journals aimed at nonacademics. Case studies are common in practitioner-oriented journals in education, social work, counseling, psychology, and business.

Sample Abstract

This sample abstract describes the therapeutic journey of Leigh (not his real name), a nine-year-old boy who was referred for play therapy due to difficulties he was having after the death of his fifteen-year-old brother. The play therapy was offered through a joint project called "Playing Through Loss" and was run jointly between a UK university and the local branch of a national bereavement organization. The project was set up to offer play therapy to bereaved children in the local area. Leigh had eight sessions of therapy and this paper describes the major themes of his play and makes some preliminary explorations of the meaning the play may have had for him. Interestingly, some of his play focused on a computer game called *Zelda*; an exploration of the powerfulness of this game as a therapeutic tool is also explored. The therapist's theoretic orientation is described along with her perceived role as "loyal companion." Finally, the process by which Leigh worked with his loss is discussed. (Robson, 2008)

PRACTICE WISDOM

Contributing to the collective body of research in your discipline is admirable. Research and other articles geared primarily for scholars are to be valued and cherished. However, often articles produced for practitioners in the fields in which we teach count among some of the most important work we can do. Sometimes faculty see teaching as service to future practitioners, but they neglect to understand that they can write scholarship for practitioners as well. I (Rich) have written several articles that stemmed from my finding that there were no adequate published articles on a topic to which I believed my students should be exposed.

Practice wisdom articles are similar in several ways to case studies. We use our own general practice experiences as a type of case example. We discuss what we did in practice, how that worked, and how that relates to theory and other approaches. Writing for practitioners is a joy. I (Rich) am free to explore topics that are important to me, and I am writing freely and without constraint. When writing practice wisdom articles, we are allowed to include ourselves more than in other types of articles. Think of writing practice wisdom articles as an extended communication between you and former students.

Sample Abstract

This article explores a new paradigm or model for the professional social worker: the poet-practitioner. The training and practice of the poet are congruent with many aspects of social work practice. An examination of the practice of the poet and the congruence of these practices to social work reveal a paradigm with the capacity to focus social workers on the essential values of our profession. This paradigm, which highlights the humanistic, creative, and socially conscience role of the social work practitioner, may be particularly important today, given the medicalization of social problems and the conservitization of society. (Furman, Langer, & Anderson, 2006)

It is possible to write more than one article about the same topic. For instance, you may craft a second article for a different audience or perhaps focus on a different aspect of the same issue or problem.

When writing from the same set of data or about a topic multiple times, you must be careful to create scholarship that is substantially different from that of past articles. Each article you write should make a unique contribution.

LITERATURE REVIEW

Intensive literature reviews are articles that explore the state of the art of a given topic and how the literature has explored the topic. Literature reviews are not merely a distillation of the available literature: they constitute an exploration of the historical trends in regard to a given subject. Literature review articles expand what is known about a topic in several key ways, and if they are successful they have several elements in common: (1) they are comprehensive, (2) they draw connections among the various studies and articles that are explored, and (3) they put forth new perspectives based on an in-depth exploration.

Successful literature reviews, like other types of articles, are carefully crafted for a particular audience. Some are geared toward policy makers, others are of value to researchers and academics, and still others are geared toward practitioners.

Sample Abstract

In order to better prepare preservice teachers for potential challenges in their first year of teaching, it is critical for both teacher educators and supervising teachers to provide strategies to strengthen preservice teachers' beliefs and maintain their motivation. In this article, strengths-based theories are reviewed to provide a discussion on teacher mentoring approaches that offer an alternative to the more common problem-based models. A strengths-based mentoring model in teacher education is presented, and measures and strategies developed from different strengths-based theories are applied to the six elements of this model. (He, 2009)

DESCRIPTIONS OF PRACTICE

Descriptions of practice demonstrate how certain techniques and methods are used with different populations, situations, and challenges. Descriptions of practice are written with practitioners in mind.

Sample Abstract

The arts and humanities have long held an important place in social work. Following from this tradition, this article explores the uses of children's literature in social work practice and education. The article explores theoretical issues that provide a rationale for using children's literature, borrowing from the insights of the field of bibliotherapy. Case studies of practice situations using specific children's books are explored. Sample exercises for teaching across the social work curriculum are also provided. (Collins, Furman, & Bruce, 2005)

THEORETICAL FORMULATIONS

One of the consequences in the trend toward valuing only data-based scholarship is the decrease of theoretical articles in the human services professions. This is lamentable, as theory is what helps bridge the gap between research and practice, and is what helps researchers and practitioners alike develop innovations. Theoretical articles often start by setting forth a theory and then explore a topic through the lens of that theory.

There are many creative, evocative ways to write theoretical articles. Many begin with an exploration of a given theory and explore how that theory can help us understand individual or social problems. Some authors demonstrate how a given theory can be applied to a particular client population or service context. Others create new theories and explore how they lend insights to a particular problem. Some theoretical articles compare and contrast how various theories inform the understanding of a phenomenon. One such article I (Rich) wrote explores depression through the lenses of two sociological theories and two psychologically oriented theories (Furman & Bender, 2003). The abstract for this article illustrates how I weaved together various components of the article.

Sample Abstract

The purpose of this paper is to discuss the social problem of depression from a multitheoretical perspective. It explores depression through the lens of two psychologically based theories of human behavior, existential theory and cognitive theory, as well as through the vehicle of two sociological theories, Marxist theory and the theory of oppression. By understanding how each of these theories explains depression, social workers may be helped to see the complexity of treating the problem. It is the belief of the authors that social work literature, which is often dominated by reductionistic, quantitatively based research studies, has increasingly ignored theoretical explorations of key social problems such as depression, to the detriment of the profession and the disciplines that inform it. (Furman & Bender, 2003, p. 123)

POLICY STUDIES

Each discipline in the human services affects and is affected by social policies and the manner in which such policies are implemented at the community, state, federal, and organizational levels. Policies affect the context of the care we provide and provide practitioners with guidance.

Sample Abstract

Topic: This paper discusses wraparound services, individualized, community-based mental health services for children in their homes and schools, that have become an integral component of the service delivery system in many states for children with severe emotional and behavioral disorders.

Purpose: The purpose of this paper is to conduct an analysis of the social policy antecedents that culminated in wraparound services in one state. The development of one state's implementation and relevant value issues are also considered.

Sources: Policy and historical literature are used to lend text to the discussion. An extensive literature review found no data regarding the effectiveness or impact of wraparound services. Therefore, experiential and anecdotal data taken from the first author's experience as a director of a large wraparound program is tentatively offered. (Furman & Jackson, 2002)

TEACHING AND PEDAGOGY

Teaching and pedagogy articles explore various teaching methods and techniques. While these articles can be based on research, they often have more of a show-and-tell or descriptive nature. That is, they present descriptions of teaching methodologies and innovations that the authors have used. Such articles may be particularly effective when written for cross-disciplinary audiences.

Sample Abstract

The purpose of this article is to demonstrate how exercises associated with poetry and bibliotherapy can be useful in assisting faculty of the helping professions teach empathy to their students. A brief exploration of the concept of empathy is discussed. Next, exercises useful in teaching empathy are presented. Finally, a case study of the work of social work students is presented to illuminate uses of exercises for teaching this important concept and skill. (Furman, 2005)

AUTOETHNOGRAPHY

As previously stated, traditional scientific writing is often impersonal. In traditional studies, researchers systematically observe the subject and attempt to write about it as objectively as possible. Yet many authors question whether such objectivity is at all possible (Ellis & Flaherty, 1992; Stein, 2004). Such authors argue that all research is interpretative in nature, and that the subjective experience of the researcher is always present in the findings. Instead of attempting to deny or mitigate the impact of the subjective understanding, many researchers bring the researcher into the research, openly explicating their own values, biases, and opinions (Eisner, 1991). Others have taken this one step farther, deciding that the researcher him- or herself is a valuable subject of research (Alsop, 2002; Ellis & Bouchner, 2000).

Sample Abstract

This performative autoethnography uses jazz swing as a method to further activate the critical processes in qualitative research. In reflecting on my father's twenty-five years as a jazz musician, I find his everyday lived methodology of swing provides an opportunity to explore the ways in which family inheritance collides with sociocultural practices of racial inequity and cultural appropriation. Autoethnographically re/inhabiting this space and sound with my father revealed a performative ethos, an empathetic epistemology of critical reflection activated by the transgressive discipline of jazz. Specifically, this performative ethos is applied to issues of racial accountability, embodied theorizing, and the ethical implications of an aesthetic/epistemic praxis in autoethnography. More broadly, I offer performative ethos as critical pedagogy assisting in living a critical life where issues of power and privilege are personally political and are written and rewritten daily with others in hope of utopia. (Spry, 2010)

ARTISTIC OR CREATIVE PRESENTATIONS

Although not applicable to everyone's work, the use of artistic and creative means of presenting data and findings can be helpful in reaching diverse audiences. For instance, expressive arts researchers use different artistic media throughout the research process in order to present findings that will have an impact on an emotional level. This is especially relevant when scholars want to move people emotionally, when they seek to encourage an empathic reaction in their readers.

Sample Abstract

The idea of immersion research has been explored in various disciplines: virtual reality, interactive storytelling, art, and so on. However, most researchers focus on constraints of the hardware and software, and are less focused on the conceptual and philosophical implications of immersion and presence. This paper aims to define a certain quality of immersion that has emerged from artistic–research experiences. Overall, immersion is an integrated conscious state where mind, body, and environment are well interrelated and interweaved. Within the concept of immersion, we explore four categories: ambient immersive natural space, body interaction, new consciousness, and flow of energy. Finally, the paper presents examples of our art based-research and offers detailed explorations on the quality of immersion. (Seo & Gromala, 2007)

LETTERS TO THE EDITOR

Writing letters to the editor can be a valuable first step in publishing your work and a good way to break into the top-ranked journals. With letters to the editor, authors engage editors and readers about ideas about articles that were previously published in the journal, or about important issues of the day or new and upcoming trends. Some letters to the editor are based in professional literature, but others are more direct opinions and comments. Here are some basic guidelines and options to consider when writing a letter to the editor (for an example, see appendix C).

1. Engage in an informed conversation about the ideas presented in an article.
2. Discuss an event of importance and its implications to society, your profession, or a select, relevant group.
3. Make a suggestion to a journal about its overall content.
4. Explore your agreement, disagreement, or a bit of both about an article or editorial position presented in the journal.
5. Connect to an important point or two from the literature, some seminal thinker, or an important professional value or concept.

BOOK REVIEWS

Book reviews are another good way to gain confidence and begin to build experience and a track record of publications. They are normally not considered peer-reviewed publications, so they should only constitute a small component of a tenure-track faculty's scholarship. However, they often are scholars' first publications. Journals that include book reviews tend to fall into two categories: those that accept unsolicited reviews and those that do not. Journals usually discuss the parameters of what they require for book reviews on authors' guidelines sections of their websites or in the journal itself. In general, book reviews range from two to five pages and discuss the strengths and weaknesses of a book, the populations for which the book is appropriate, and the general importance of the book. When writing a book review, you want to contextualize the book with other ideas and publications within your professional field.

Sample Abstract

The frequency with which I have discussed or quoted from this book with colleagues underlines its usefulness. Hawton and Rodham provide an account of an international survey of deliberate self-harm and suicidal thinking among adolescents. There is evidence that the majority of suicide attempts go undetected and untreated. The community-based study asked thousands of young people in five European countries and Australia about their experiences of self-harm. The findings are discussed across nine chapters presented in two parts. (Teggart, 2009)

QUANTITATIVE STUDIES

We have left quantitative studies for the end, as this is what many of us tend to view as publishable research. The best way to decide how to structure a quantitative article is to read the journals in your disciplines and subdisciplines. Quantitative articles tend to follow similar formats: an introduction, a literature review that provides a rationale for the topic area (including how the present study fills gaps in current knowledge), methodology, findings and results, discussion, implications, and conclusion. Quantitative research tends to be a highly structured linear process, and so quantitative articles tend to follow suit. This makes sense, because the design of an article may naturally follow the logic of the inquiry.

Types of Publications to Approach with Caution

Submitting writing for publication in peer-reviewed journals is a long process, as described at length in chapter 6. Some may be tempted to skip that route and publish by any means necessary, for example submitting work to nonrefereed websites or even self-publishing a book. Although this may seem like a good solution to save time, there are several disadvantages. Publishing in nonrefereed sources may seem like a surefire way to disseminate your ideas, but your work will not be included in academic search databases. As such, you will reach a smaller audience. If a goal of publishing is to add a line to your CV, you may be doing yourself a disservice if your only publication is one that has not been refereed. It may communicate that you were not willing to engage in the review process or that the writing was not of high quality. Finally, the peer-review process simply does not take that much more work than submitting to a nonrefereed source. Although you may face a higher rejection rate, the feedback you receive can be an invaluable resource to help you improve.

Exercise 12

WANDERING THROUGH
THE STACKS

Spend several hours at the library of the best research university in your area. We suggest you go to one with which you are not familiar. This will add a sense of mystery and adventure to your quest. Take your academic notebook with you (and if you have not yet created one, now would be a good time to do so).

For several hours, wander the stacks of journals. Start with journals that are not in your discipline, that perhaps are not even related to your discipline. As you wander the stacks, pull out journals that catch your eye. Flip through the tables of contents to see if any article appears interesting, for whatever reason. Try to find articles that are different, methodologically speaking, from those you have seen before. Try to find articles that have an interesting tone or are constructed in a manner with which you are not familiar. Read the abstracts and perhaps the first page of those articles. Without pressuring yourself to come up with anything, ask yourself if any of these articles relate to your work. Are the authors doing anything that you may consider doing? Let yourself think freely, and do not censor your thoughts. Jot down your answers to these questions, or just jot down whatever thoughts are triggered during your search. After you have done this for a while, sit down in a quiet, comfortable area of the library and write out what you have learned.

Note: It has been brought to my attention that some young scholars today may resist the notion of actually doing research without the aid of a computer. We urge you to push yourselves to try this technique, as Paleolithic as it may seem.

Exercise 13

WRITING TWO ABSTRACTS

Choose two types of articles from the last chapter, preferably ones that you have not previously considered writing about. Thinking of an important research interest, try to come up with the title and abstracts for the articles. Abstracts are synopses of articles that include each of the key components addressed. Be as creative as you can, and for now do not think about the feasibility of the research. It is important to allow your mind to come up with different possibilities. If you like, work out a potential plan for the design of each article.

Chapter 5

SELECTING A JOURNAL

Selection of a journal may seem like a cut-and-dried decision, but it is actually anything but. The selection is an important process that can mean the difference between success and failure. A few introductory points may help provide some context. While you may already have an article written and are now looking for an appropriate journal, to the degree possible it is advisable for several reasons to write subsequent articles after you have selected a target journal and to select additional journals as backups. First, by selecting your target journal prior to writing or early on in the process, you will be able to write to a particular audience. Second, you will know exactly the style and the particular idiosyncrasies of the journal. Some journals will follow the guidelines of the *APA Style Manual* (American Psychological Association [APA], 2009), while others will use the Chicago Style Manual (University of Chicago, 2010). Some journals will follow other writing conventions. At times, journals even follow parts of one style but use their own guidelines for other parts of the process. Third, you will be able to explore the work of authors who have been published in the journal before and include some of these authors in your citations.

I view journal selection as one of the first (and most critical) steps to transforming a research project into an article. Selecting a journal at the beginning of the writing process is helpful because it allows me to target the framing of my argument to the journal's audience. If I'm writing an article for a developmental psychology journal, I'll approach the framing in a different way than if I'm writing it for a community psychology journal. I usually start by compiling a short list of journals that might be receptive to the topic, theoretical orientation, and analyses included in my research project. To create this list, I often look at the articles that I am planning to cite to see where they were published. I also ask colleagues if they have any thoughts about journals that might be a good fit for my work. Next, with my short list in hand, I explore journal websites and the Web of Science to gather more information. Here, I generally look at the journal's aims and scope, who sits on the editorial board, and the impact factor. I have also emailed editors to ask about turnaround times and acceptance rates. Taking all of these factors into consideration, I'm generally able to narrow the list to my first and second choices.

Jenna Watling Neal, PhD
Michigan State University
Personal correspondence

It is important to remember that an author does not submit him- or herself for evaluation, but only a small sample of his or her work. You are not your article, and the inevitable rejection of a manuscript is not a rejection of you. At first it most certainly feels as if this were the case. Everyone who has submitted an article has felt the sting of rejection. Sometimes we use various coping mechanisms to cover up that sting, such as becoming angry at editors and reviewers. It is important to guard against these deflections, as they can hinder your establishing and maintaining of good relationships with editors. Such defensiveness also inhibits your ability to learn from the process and may lead to self-evaluations that decrease your motivation to attempt to publish your work.

SELECTING JOURNALS

Selection of a journal is a crucial decision. Many authors believe that selecting a journal comes after writing. While it is certainly possible to submit an existing article to a journal you deem appropriate, it is best to have a specific journal in mind while you are preparing your manuscript. Each journal has its own set of ideas regarding what a good article is. Some journals prefer longer and more in-depth literature review sections, while others want them to be more concise. Some journals want your article to be fewer than twenty pages, while others will accept much longer articles.

As previously mentioned, knowing the expectations for tenure at your institution is an important consideration when selecting a journal. Some departments and colleges value peer-reviewed electronic journals, and others do not. Market factors dictate that most universities over time will come to recognize the value of electronic sources of dissemination, but biases still remain. Similarly, some departments demand that you publish in specific journals. For some departments, publications that appear only in the top two or three journals of a field lead to positive tenure decisions. Fortunately, most institutions and departments are more flexible for junior faculty, allowing numerous choices for publishing an article. However, it is essential to know these expectations beforehand. If you must publish in a very selective few journals, consider it a crucial aspect of your work that you know everything you can about these journals, from the types of articles they publish to the interests of their editorial board members.

At some of the institutions with which we have been affiliated, the "impact factor" of a journal is an important criterion for evaluating the quality of a journal. The impact factor measures the average number of times that a certain article from a specific journal has been cited. While it is a deeply flawed measure of actual value (e.g., practitioners may not cite an article but use its contents in actual practice situations), the measure has been used as an indication of the merit of a journal. However, many other factors should be considered when assessing a journal. Following is a discussion of some of the key factors to think about in making your choices.

> One of the first things I do is decide whether to submit to a general journal or a specialized one. If you have a paper that has interesting but not necessarily Earth-shattering results, you might want to shoot for a journal that deals with a specific research topic, such as relationships, or emotion. Generally, as you get broader, the impact, readership, and citations increase, but so do rejection rates. A good rule of thumb for journal selection is to first make sure that your article is appropriate for the journal. Once you've narrowed your choices to a few journals, shoot for the one with the highest impact factor that you think you have a chance at. If it gets rejected, chances are you'll at least receive some good feedback for submitting it to a different journal.
>
> Michael J. Marks, PhD
> New Mexico State University
> Personal correspondence

FINDING JOURNALS

Finding and evaluating journals is an important part of the publication process. Getting to know what is out there in terms of journals is essential not only for the publication process, but also for writing. Exercise 12 hopefully will have helped you to begin this process. While this may sound old fashioned in an electronic world (and indeed, electronic sources, which we discuss shortly, are invaluable), I (Rich) cannot tell you how often flipping through journals has inspired a new article, opened up the possibility of some new way of approaching a topic, or even introduced me to a new research methodology. In fact, it was wandering through the stacks at the University of Kansas library that opened up a new methodological approach that has become one of the key areas of my scholarship. For those less inclined to such old-fashioned methods, a list of some helpful electronic sources for locating journals can be found in appendix B.

Wandering through the stacks and picking up journals that catch your eye may do several things. First, it will connect or reconnect you to the physical world of publishing. There is a huge difference between holding a journal in our hands and reading one online. The former leads to a greater degree of emotional connectedness, of relationship with the authors of the articles. Second, by wandering through the stacks, you will see journals in other fields that you may never have considered before. For instance, I have found nursing and educational journals to be wonderful sources of insight on qualitative methodology. Third, as previously mentioned, wandering through the stacks and flipping through journals can be a wonderful source of ideas and inspiration.

EVALUATING A JOURNAL

Whereas wandering through the stacks is a wonderful way to get to know journals, journal evaluation can often be done online. Most journals have a home page, usually found within the website of its publisher. A journal's home page typically has a great deal of information that will be of value to you at several points in the process. Different publishers name these sections differently, but they all typically include a statement of aims and purpose, article submission instructions or guidelines for contributors, previous tables of contents, names of editorial board members, indexing information, and other valuable information. This information is also found in some issues of print journals, usually toward the very front or the very back.

In evaluating a journal as a potential source of information, read the introductory statements about the aims and mission of the journal and ask yourself if your work is consistent with those aims. Articles frequently are rejected for not being congruent with the basic aims of the journal, even if they are excellent scholarly works. Unfortunately, editors do not always catch these incongruities early on, so if you submit your article to a journal that is ill suited for your work, you may not be made aware of this problem until the article has been reviewed many months later.

After reviewing for basic congruence, make certain that the methodology of your work is congruent with those that the journal advocates. For instance, if the journal only accepts empirical work, a theoretical article will have little chance of being accepted. Some journals are not clear about this in the guidelines they provide. If there is any doubt, look at the tables of contents of several issues to see whether your article is of the type that is typically published. If the titles listed in the tables of contents still do not give you a clear idea with regard to fit, scan the article abstracts from several issues. Even though the journal's introductory paragraphs may state that it is open to a certain type of work, editors have their biases, and what is ultimately published may be the best indication of an editor's scholarly preferences.

Should your article still seem a good fit for the journal, read through the contributors' guidelines, often also known as Instructions for Authors, or Submission Guidelines. These guidelines will further elaborate on the journal's audience, the types of articles considered, and the methodologies preferred. Guidelines usually state the desired length of acceptable articles, either in pages or words, and what content counts toward this total (e.g., some journals include references in the overall page count, while others do not). Journals often accept articles of varying lengths for different sections. For example, the *Journal of Qualitative Social Work* accepts regular articles of 4,000 to 7,000 words. The journal also has several others sections: New Voices is primarily for practitioners, graduate students, and new scholars, and allows work from 2,750 to 4,000 words; Response and Commentary includes responses to previous articles and encourages articles of 1,000 to 1,500 words; Practice and Teaching of Qualitative Social Work is a section of how-to articles, with the same length requirements as the New Voices section. New authors and graduate students may wish to try their hand at writing for journals that accept shorter articles as a means of gaining confidence and achieving initial success. Writing shorter articles is also more efficient in terms of the work required to achieve publication success and can teach us the value of parsimony.

At times, journals state what type of font or font size they prefer and the required page margins. Contributors' guidelines lay out expectations for abstracts and keywords, if required. Of particular importance is the journal's citation and reference style. Following a journal's guidelines for how references are to be displayed will save countless hours in the revision process. Many authors find the use of the computer programs such as EndNote extremely useful in formatting references.

We suggest not only that you identify the journal to which you will submit your article, but also that you identify two backup journals. While you certainly want to be positive and hope that your article is accepted for publication, at some point rejection is inevitable. Most journals only accept between 10 and 50 percent of the articles submitted; the only scholars who have not had work rejected are those who have never submitted their work. Since you have been evaluating journals, it should be easy for you to rank three journals. This task becomes more difficult when you are no longer immersed in the article and the specific criteria of each journal. Start a file for each article that you submit. In this file, include copies of the contributor's guidelines and other relevant materials that pertain to your second- and third-choice journals.

To Query or Not to Query

There are those who believe it is important to query a journal about the appropriateness of their work, while others believe that if you have done your homework well, this is an unnecessary step. We believe that if there is any doubt in your mind about the fit between your article and the journal, it is an excellent idea to send a query letter (or email, preferably). The editor's assessment of your article is crucial to your article being published.

When you send a query letter, it is a good idea to include the abstract of your article. Read your abstract carefully and make sure it provides enough information about the topic, the methodology, and the most important conclusions. You also may provide in the cover letter additional information that helps contextualize the article.

Querying may be used to understand other important factors about the journal, such as the typical length of review, any questions about the method of submission, or even the lag time between acceptance and publication. Sending a query letter also may help you determine how "author friendly," invested, and available the editor is. If you have not heard from an editor in several weeks, and your article is indeed publishable, this may be a good indication that your article might not be given the attention it deserves during the review process. We should say that editors' work is usually not compensated, and most do a wonderful job. However, some do not, and identifying journals that are less than wonderfully managed will save you a great deal of time and heartache. While it may be easier to send query letters via email, you may wish to send some queries through traditional mail. The added formality of a paper letter may be less easy for an editor to ignore.

Additional Factors to Consider in Selecting a Journal

Knowing the acceptance rate of a particular journal will help you decide whether to submit your article. Acceptance rates range from less than 10 percent of articles submitted to well over 50 percent. If you are a junior faculty member who has yet to establish a significant publication record, or if you have not published the amount needed for tenure at your institution, we recommend that you not yet submit articles to the most competitive journals. While these certainly may bring you more prestige than other journals, we believe it best to first meet your minimum publication goals. Again, make sure to understand the context of your university and department, and consult with your mentors. We are not advocating sending your work to low-quality journals— we want to be clear on that point. There are many excellent publications aside from those that are often considered the top-tier journals.

There are two basic ways to ascertain acceptance rates. The first is to consult a publication that has this information, such as *An Author's Guide to Social Work Journals* (NASW, 1997). However, you will often have to ask the editor him- or herself. Many editors are willing to provide this information; some, however, are not, and others may not have calculated their acceptance rates. In addition to merely asking about the general acceptance rate, it is helpful to ask the acceptance rate for your particular type of article. For example, the editor may be able to tell you that while the guidelines state that qualitative articles are accepted, perhaps only a very small percentage of them actually make it to the journal. As with many other issues, querying the editor may save you time and undue rejection at some point down the road.

The time it takes for your article to be reviewed varies as much as the acceptance rate and is equally important. We have had review times range from a few weeks (very rare) to nearly a year for a first review; three to six months is more typical. The difference between three and six months, however, is great. Many articles take two or more revisions to move toward publication, so lengthy review times can be problematic. For an article that is rejected, it is better to know quickly and to send it to another journal than to have it tied up in a lengthy review process.

Summer reviews are another consideration. Some journals are much slower in the summer or do not even review at all during that time. This is important information to consider if you are submitting near the end of the academic calendar.

Scholarship that is cutting edge today may not be cutting edge three years down the line. A policy analysis that has clear social relevance in 2009 may not have the same currency in 2011. The lag time to publication—the length of time that it takes to bring your article from acceptance to publication—is an important consideration for prospective authors. For some types of articles, lengthy publication waiting periods may not be an issue. Again, editors are the primary source of information about waiting periods. However, it is also true that sometimes editors will tell prospective authors their ideal lag time, not the actual lag time. Consult with others who have published in the journal. In some journals, the date of submission and the date of acceptance are printed after the article; this information allows you to see how long the journal takes to process typical articles (notwithstanding how long it takes for authors to review their work).

Depending on your stage of career, lag times to publication may have different implications. For example, if you are currently a graduate student or a new PhD looking for a faculty position, you may need a printed article to send along with your curriculum vitae. Targeting journals with relatively short review periods and lag times may allow you to have more material to use in your job search.

The technological revolution that is the Internet and cyberspace has led to powerful changes in the way scholarly communication is and will be published. Peer-reviewed electronic journals are becoming increasingly popular throughout academia. The trend toward developing open-access journals, those published on the World Wide Web that are free to all, has become something of a social movement. Open-access journals pride themselves on maintaining the rigor of print journals while providing a more egalitarian access to information. Although today they are far from achieving acceptance in many academic circles, scholarly electronic journals may one day become the norm.

Although some may lament the trend, peer-reviewed electronic journals have several advantages over print journals for publishers, consumers, and authors alike. Electronic journals tend to be far less costly and far less time consuming than print journals to produce. Since they are less costly to produce, journals that do charge are sometimes less costly for the consumer, unless a commercial publisher has chosen to increase its profit margin. As previously stated, many electronic academic journals are free, open to anyone who can access the Internet. This allows for wider dissemination of research results and ideas. Also, electronic journals can sometimes accept articles with audio and video materials as part of the articles themselves, leading to potentially new and exciting ways to present research results. Such multimedia presentations provide scholars with new ways to conceptualize their research.

For authors, there are several practical advantages of electronic journals. First, review times are often shortened because of time that would otherwise be spent in the traditional mail system. Typically, authors send their article to the editor electronically, and the editor in turn will send the article to reviewers in the same format. The article is then returned electronically to the editor, who submits the reviewers' comments to you via email. It is easy to see how electronic submissions can save nearly a month in the review process. It should be noted that print journals increasingly have created mechanisms for electronic submissions, thereby saving time in their review processes as well.

Once an article is accepted to an electronic journal, the lag time between acceptance and publication is usually shorter than it is with print journals. There are two reasons for this. First, since electronic journals are still gaining acceptance, they might not receive as many submissions as some print journals, although this can vary greatly. Some online journals receive far more articles than they can use. More significant, electronic journals do not have the same space limitations as print journals do. An editor can include nearly as many articles as he or she wishes in one volume. We have had several articles published in peer-reviewed electronic journals six months to a year after the original submission date. Conversely, it is not uncommon for articles to be published in print journals several years after they were initially sent for review. Some electronic journals may be the best place for time-sensitive material.

Chapter 6

SUBMITTING YOUR MANUSCRIPT

Now that you have selected a journal, we need to focus on the details of the submission process. We begin with discussion of the importance of your relationship and work with journal editors.

EDITORS ARE PEOPLE TOO

How often do we hear that academia is political? We throw around this slogan but often do not have a clear idea of what it means. Sometimes we understand that for junior faculty this means not angering those who have the power within departments or schools. We are taught to serve on certain committees, to make ourselves visible to the right people, and not to make waves. We (Julie and Rich) believe that there is a less nefarious and more positive spin on the meaning of academic politics. To me (Rich), politics is learning how to negotiate systems and learning who has power, and how to interact with those in power. Ultimately, it means treating all your colleagues well.

An example from my (Rich's) experience will serve. I submitted an article to a well-known journal in my discipline. Several months went by, and I did not hear from the editor. I sent an email but did not hear back. I sent a letter. Finally, I heard back. It seemed that the editor was preoccupied with supporting a close friend in a time of need. My article took a backseat. I genuinely felt bad for her, offered my support, and let her know that my article was clearly secondary and that she should take her time. Further, I asked her if there was anything I could do. Simple and human. Now fast-forward a few months: after a second revision, my article was rejected. All told, the article was out for review in this journal for more than a year and was then rejected. In fact, I believed the rejection was somewhat arbitrary and that the reasons given were not issues I had been asked to address. Was I angry and disappointed? Of course, but what good would expressing my anger have done? While righteous indignation is a wonderfully addictive feeling, it rarely gets us anywhere. Instead, I thanked the editor for her time and effort and told her I would love to submit an article in the future. She wrote me back thanking me for my understanding. One fewer bridges burned, one more door opened.

Editors make many important decisions in the process and you are not usually anonymous to them, only to the reviewers. Many journals now require electronic submission, which can reduce editors' access to your identifying information. However, blind review may be impossible in small research communities. We often know a great deal about our colleagues' projects and can pinpoint a research team based on a unique method or approach.

Editors are like the rest of us. We go out of the way for those we respect and enjoy, and we try to minimize contact with those we do not. Understanding the experience and role of the editor in the peer-review process can be helpful. A senior colleague once told me that schmoozing editors was not important in the blind-review process. We strongly disagree. First, they decide if the article is worth sending out for review. If an editor is negatively predisposed against you, he or she has the choice to not send your article out or merely deem that it does "not meet the needs of the journal at this time." Further, it is the editor who decides which reviewers will evaluate your article. All journals are not equal, and neither are reviewers. Establish a good relationship with an editor and your article is more likely to wind up in the hands of a good reviewer, one who is efficient and helpful.

Also, it is the editor who makes the final decision about publication. The reviewer's comments are recommendations, not laws sent down from the mountain. It is the editor who decides what feedback from the reviewers you should pay attention to. The editor even decides whether corrections should be sent back to the original reviewers or if the editor will be responsible for reviewing revisions. Recently, in response to conflicting statements made by several reviewers, an editor informed me that to make our lives "easier," she was going to review subsequent changes. She even carefully differentiated between changes she believed were most essential and those that were optional.

PEER REVIEW

We have discussed peer-reviewed publications without defining what peer review is. While many readers may be familiar with peer review, a discussion of some of peer review's dynamics might be of value. Peer review is also referred to as refereed or blind review. First, peer review, as the name indicates, is conducted by peers, usually scholars, experts, or practitioners in the journal's field of study. The peers serve as referees or evaluators for the articles. Usually, two or three referees are asked to evaluate the article on a number of criteria, which we address later. Reviews are blind: that is, reviewers do not know the name of the submitting author. This helps ensure that decisions are based on the merits of the article, not on political or other issues. Peer review has long been an important feature of scholarly publication for various reasons. First, before the Internet, when print journals were the only source of scholarly publication available, space in scholarly publications was finite (Odlyzko, 1995). Peer review became a means of conserving valuable space. Second, peer review serves to weed out unsound scholarship.

THE DETAILS OF SUBMISSION

Once you have selected your journal, carefully read then reread the guidelines for authors. You should follow these important instructions to the letter, unless you received more up-to-date information from an editor that contradicts some of these instructions. When discrepancies exist, it is best to clarify any point with the editor.

Typically, you will be asked to submit between three and five copies of your article with identifying information on only one of the copies. One copy with the title of the article and the name and contact information of the first author and the names and affiliations of subsequent authors will go to the editor. The other copies usually require only a title page, without author information. Pay attention to the little details while preparing your manuscript for submission. While it is true that you are not your manuscript and that you should not overly attach yourself to your work in the review process, it is also true that your manuscript represents you. Therefore, you want to make sure that you handle every detail professionally. This will mean that the copies of your manuscript should all be laser-printed copies. Do not use dot-matrix or even ink-jet printers if you can help it. Make certain that each copy contains all the pages and that all pages are of good quality. Make sure that you submit your cover letter and articles in large manila envelopes, and do not stuff your work into a normal or business-size envelope. Use good paper clips or staples for your article, and attach your cover page with a small binder clip. Of course, these are only general guidelines; be sure to follow the journal's instructions.

Abstract

Most journals require an abstract of between 75 and 200 words. Since the abstract is the reviewers' introduction to your article, it is best to take some care in its creation. Too often, the abstract is written as a last-minute addition and is not given the same attention as the rest of the article. As with all material that you submit, make sure to ask a colleague to carefully read your abstract.

Journals often ask for keywords to be included. Keywords are single words or phrases used for abstracting as well as for database retrieval purposes. Select keywords that cover the subject, methodology, and interest area of your article.

Cover Letters

Cover letters also demand attention, but they are all too often neglected. The cover letter may not be the first communication you have with the editor, but it is certainly one of the earliest. Cover letters should be short, humble, helpful, and personal to the degree possible. Cover letters should rarely be more than two paragraphs in length if you do not have a significant personal relationship with the editor. The first sentence should tell the editor the title of the article you are sending and the number of copies, and the name of the journal. If you had previous contact with the editor about the article, reference that communication early in the letter. While it is certainly permissible to tell the editor that you believe your article would be an excellent match for his or her journal, it might not be in your best interest to say, for example, that your article will change the very nature of the profession. (For a sample submission cover letter, see appendix D.)

MANAGING THE REVIEW PROCESS

What do you do once you have mailed your article? Well, you wait, of course. But there are important steps to take during the wait. First, it is important that you reward yourself for completing an important task. You have completed something that will hopefully lead to a professional contribution. Do something nice for yourself that signifies an achievement. The temptation is to only reward oneself for the acceptance of an article. However, we believe it is more important to reward yourself for your hard work. Engaging in the process and making the effort will get you to your publication goals. Being invested in the outcome will only slow you down in the process, as getting an article accepted for publication is a slow and often an arduous process. Rewarding your efforts, however, will help you make your writing and scholarship an important ritual in your life.

After you have given yourself your reward, keep up your momentum and begin working on your next project. As we previously discussed, we believe that it is important to work on more than one article at a time: you can do different tasks on each one, depending on your mood. The key is to keep writing and working consistently over time. So, now you have been waiting and some time has passed. Many wonder if you wait idly for the editor to get back to you or if you can contact the editor. After several weeks, the editor should have acknowledged his or her receipt of your article. It is fair to contact him or her via email if you have not received any contact, politely asking if he or she has received your work. The next contact with the editor—provided, of course, that you have not received reviews—is at the anticipated date that the journal expects a review to be completed. Often, in his or her acknowledgement letter, the editor will inform you of the anticipated review time. If you did not previously inquire and do not know when the editor expects to have received reviews, it is fair to query about the status of your article three to four months after it was submitted. Remember that editors and reviewers are extremely busy people, usually faculty or practitioners like you. When you contact the editor about your article and your reviews still have not been received, the editor will usually contact the reviewers and ask about the status of your article. A respectful note can serve as a friendly reminder.

REVISIONS

You find a letter from the journal in your mailbox. Brace yourself: your article most likely has not been accepted as is for publication. I (Rich) have only had one article ever accepted with no revisions. This is very rare. Consider that reviewers are highly skilled professionals whose training, personality, and ideas are not identical to yours. At the very least, they will have suggested some changes to your article, so prepare yourself for some degree of rejection.

When you open the envelope, you will find a letter from the editor that informs you of several potential outcomes of the review process. Different journals have different categories of potential decision, but they tend to be very similar. First is "accepted with no revisions." Again, this is very rare and usually only happens on an article that has been rejected previously, worked on extensively, and submitted to a new journal. The best to realistically hope for is the decision to "accept with minor revisions." This means that your article has been accepted, provided that you make the necessary changes. Depending on how minor the changes really are and depending on the journal, your article may or may not go back for a second review. Typically, once the article has been accepted on this level, the editor will make sure that the requested changes have been made. If it does go back out for review, the understanding is that the reviewers will only look to check that you made their suggested revisions.

A more common decision is to "revise and resubmit," which in the letter may be expressed as either "reject," "revise and resubmit," "revise with major revisions," or something to that effect. Do not despair at this decision, as it signifies that the reviewers and the editor believe that your work has merit and that with changes it may be publishable. We have seen many practitioners and new scholars react to this decision with a sense of defeat. They have worked so hard on their manuscript but now are being told it is not good enough. Instead of despairing, celebrate! You have passed the first test and are well on the way to having your article published—if not in this journal, then most certainly in another. Remember what we firmly believe: "If you write it, it will be published."

This can be true for you as well. Perhaps you will not publish in the first journal that you submit an article to, and perhaps not even the second. One of the best articles that I (Rich) wrote (in my opinion) was rejected four times before it was finally accepted. When it was finally accepted, almost no revisions were needed, and the editor was as positive about my work as the previous editors had been negative. In times like this it is best to think of publishing as a game (albeit a very important and valuable game), and not a personal judgment. It is a game that demands a great deal of patience and perseverance, but one at which everyone can eventually win.

The last potential decision is a straight rejection without an invitation to resubmit your work. Again, you are not your work, so be careful and do not personalize the decision. It was only your article that was rejected, not you.

Along with a rejection decision letter, you will most likely be provided with feedback from the reviewers. The identity of the reviewers has been masked, for their protection! What you think about the feedback will often depend on the decision. Before we discuss how to use this feedback, remember this: you have been given an extraordinary gift. You have been given professional consultation for free. The reviewers provided feedback to you as a professional service, as a courtesy that you will return to others in your role as a reviewer (a key aspect of your professional development, to be covered later). If the decision is highly positive, reading the feedback will be easy. If your article was rejected, this may not be painless. Try to read the feedback first without evaluating it: just read it and let it wash over you. If the feedback is particularly difficult, we suggest that you put it away for a day or two and come back to it. Notice, we said only a day or two. You have important decisions to make, and this is not the time for long-term inaction. This is a particularly vulnerable time for you as an author; you must fight the tendency to be discouraged and to give up hope. You must stay in action. The two actions that will serve you well are continuing to work on other writing projects and using the two-week resubmission rule. The two-week resubmission rule is a good rule of thumb for the best time frame for sending a rejected article to a new journal. Often, articles that are rejected sit in a closed drawer for months on end, with the author waiting for the time to revise and resubmit the work. Too often, the time never arrives. Therefore, after a day or two of cooling-off time, we go back to the reviewers' feedback. Try to be as nondefensive as possible, and ask, "What can I gain from the feedback to improve my article?" Other useful questions to ask yourself include, "What points do they make that are valid? What changes can I make based on their feedback that will help me develop as a scholar?" Then ask yourself if you are willing to make these changes within the next two weeks. If so, we suggest you sit down to revise the article and send it to the backup journal that you previously selected. However, if you do not believe that the reviewers have merit, or if you cannot imagine working on the article at this time, we suggest you send it back to a different journal right away. At this point, you may wonder if you are setting yourself up for more rejection by sending out a flawed article. We have found that often new reviewers from a different journal will give entirely different feedback, sometimes feedback that is more helpful but other times not. When feedback is not different, when there is a high level of congruence between the two sets of reviews, you have to strongly consider what they are saying. You must follow a different set of procedures on an article that has been designated "revise and resubmit." Although usually it is wise to make the suggested changes and resubmit your article, there are times when it may not be in your best interest to do so.

What you must change in the revision processes is defined in one of two ways: either the editor tells you what aspects of the reviewers' suggestions you must take or the editor informs you that you must make the suggested changes. In either case, if you agree with or at least see merit in the suggested changes, then by all means make all of them. If you find that some of the reviewers' comments may be difficult to consider, or you do not agree with them, this may be the time to send an email to the editor asking for his or her advice. The editor may tell you that you do need to make the changes should you want your article to be considered, or the editor may understand your perspective and encourage you to make as many changes as you feel appropriate. Should this be the case, you will need to discuss your reasons for not making a change in your resubmission cover letter (see appendix E).

At times, while reading your feedback you may find that one or two of your reviews were generally positive (yet may still ask for considerable revision) but that one reviewer had a particularly negative tone. It is important to pay attention to this. Ask yourself if the reviewer seems to be negatively predisposed to your article. Is there any indication that the reviewer may not be swayed no matter what changes you make? Remember, one of your reviewers may have voted against your being able to revise your article and may be very negative about it. At this point, you may ask a colleague to read and assess the feedback. If your colleague believes that the feedback is excessively negative, you may again want to explore this issue with the editor. On more than one occasion I (Rich) have voiced concern with an editor about a reviewer's feedback and have asked whether all the original reviewers would need to reassess the article. At times, editors have informed me that each reviewer will review the article, but the editor recognizes that the reviewer may be less positive than the others. You may want to attach the emails with your cover letter and articles when you resubmit, so the editor remembers your exchange. In situations such as this, we are very open and clear with the editor with regard to exploring the nature of the changes to be made and the changes that we feel are inappropriate. On the basis of the editor's response, we can decide whether we want to resubmit the article or try another journal.

One difficult experience that I frequently encounter is when a reviewer (or worse, an editor) asks you to do something that is, in an objective sense, incorrect. One topic where I consistently encounter this type of scenario is the presentation of statistics using p-values. Traditionally, many researchers interpret or imply that p-values are effect sizes, which they are not. To give a concrete example, I've been asked many times to "provide either exact p-values or the p-value at the 'highest level of significance' so readers can get a sense of how strong the effect is." I've found the most constructive way to handle this kind of scenario is to come up with an educational compromise, one that allows you to still be correct, yet will satisfy (and maybe even enlighten) the editor or reviewer. With the p-value scenario, I will often report exact p-values (e.g., "$p < .001$" instead of using a firm alpha cutoff such as .05), but will also caution the reader that "as p-values are not effect sizes, we include [measure of appropriate effect size] for comparisons of effect size." After encountering this scenario several times, I now preemptively remind the readers that p-values are not effect sizes. I haven't had a request for exact values since.

Michael J. Marks, PhD
New Mexico State University
Personal correspondence

When you do resubmit your article, a new cover letter is important (for samples of resubmission cover letters, see appendixes E and F). In this letter, you want to first thank the editor and the reviewers for their time, hard work, and valuable feedback. You may also wish to state how grateful you are for their help and that you believe their insights have helped you improve your article. We also like to state that we see the process of publication as a collaborative venture between the reviewers, editor, and ourselves, and that we would be glad to make subsequent changes to the article, if need be. We believe this helps to create a spirit of collaboration between colleagues, which is indeed what the process should be. Oftentimes, editors are treated as gate-keepers, but this is not an effective stance. Remember, editors are colleagues who are performing an invaluable service to their profession at no cost. The role of editors is to help facilitate the integration of the best and most relevant ideas and research into their profession.

Next, carefully state how you went about incorporating the reviewers' comments into your article. If you can, state exactly where in the article you made changes. For more pervasive corrections that occur throughout the article, explain how you made your changes. The goal is to be able to communicate to the editor and the reviewers that you have made at the very least a good-faith effort to incorporate the changes and, at best, have fully integrated the spirit of their suggestions. It is important also to note and clearly explain any suggested changes that you did not make.

Don't take reviews personally. They can sometimes be painful, but more times than not they will make your paper much stronger. Persistence is the biggest key to publishing. So, if your manuscript is rejected after an initial submission, spend some time addressing the reviews and promptly send it back out to your second choice journal. If your manuscript receives a revise and resubmit, even better! Carefully address the reviewers' comments and make sure to craft a killer cover letter that shows how you tackled each of their critiques.

Jenna Watling Neal, PhD
Michigan State University
Personal correspondence

NOT AGAIN!

It is very possible that when you receive your next response from the editor, you will be asked to make additional revisions. Again, this is good news: it means that your article is still in the game and has not been rejected. This can be frustrating at times, as you may find that you are asked to make changes that could have been identified previously. Before you give in to the temptations to call the editor and report what an incompetent so-and-so the reviewer is, take a deep breath and remember your goal: to publish in that journal. Also, remember that editors and reviewers are busy people, too. They are human and make mistakes. As with the previous request for revisions, carefully consider your options and move forward.

On the other hand, you may receive additional feedback and corrections that, while substantive, are clearly of a lesser magnitude than during the first review. You might even start to get a sense of whether the process is progressing well. If they are, make your revisions again and follow the same process as for resubmission. If not, follow the guidelines given previously. The next review period should be much shorter.

AFTER ALL THAT, REJECTION?

It happens. You carefully and painstakingly made all the requested revisions. You may even have had a colleague read your article and cross-check the changes you made. Yet at times your article still may be rejected. This can happen for any number of reasons. A reviewer may no longer be with the journal or may be too busy to review, so the editor sends your work to a new person. Perhaps the original reviewer was not very positive about your article in the first place, yet you were not able to pick up on this in the review process. Or perhaps the editor realized at this late stage that your article really is not a good match for the journal, at least at this time. At this point, consider any additional feedback you may have been given and immediately make any changes to the document that you wish to make. When you have made these changes (if any), send the article immediately to the backup journal you have selected.

UPON ACCEPTANCE

Finally, the letter arrives that you have been waiting for. Your article has been accepted! There are several important things to do. First, celebrate! Second, celebrate! Third, celebrate! We rarely spend enough time rejoicing in our accomplishments and those of our colleagues. You will also need to immediately share the good news with your coauthors (if you have any). It is also advisable to contact those who helped you in the process, perhaps colleagues who read your manuscript or helpful librarians, and thank them for their contribution to your work. You can also include their names in your article's acknowledgment section, provided that the journal allows for this, and give them a copy once the article has been published.

Before you get totally swept up in the tide of joy, remember that you still have some work to do. In your acceptance letter, you will be asked to provide copies of the article, perhaps on disk, and there may be some forms to complete, including a transfer of copyright. This is usually a template form with space for the title of your article and the names of all the authors. Transferring copyright provides the journal almost all distribution rights to the work. Essentially, only the publisher can now decide how the completed work will be used (and how it will earn the publisher money). Although this may seem absolute, most publishers allow authors to maintain some rights to the work. For example, the author usually can post the final work to his or her personal website, can present the work at conferences, and can derive future writing from the article. If the article includes a new technique, procedure, or measure, the author maintains the right to patent or trademark. It may feel awkward to transfer the copyright. If the journal's website does not provide specific information about the rights you will retain, it is perfectly acceptable to ask questions before you sign the form.

Recently, some publishers have ceased requiring authors to assign them copyright. Instead, they ask authors to grant the publisher license to publish. This agreement indicates that only the publisher can publish the specific work, but that the author maintains all other rights. The author does not need to ask permission to use the article. Typically, when using a license to publish approach, the author is expected to submit the completed work to a scholarly repository after six months (e.g., the public website for the author's institution or the funding source). This movement in part derives from the 2001 Zwolle conference, an international collaboration to increase dissemination of scholarly work while protecting intellectual property (Crews & Westrienen, 2007). By using a license to publish, the journal can still make money by publishing the article, but the author can more broadly help disseminate his or her ideas.

You also may have been asked to make some additional changes to the work. Within a couple of months before your article is published, a copy editor who works for the publisher will most likely contact you. Typically, you are given a week to respond to any problems with the article that occur at this stage. For example, copy editors rarely address substantive changes but will point out grammatical errors or problems with your references.

If you were careful in checking your references, these may be minimal. However, it is a good idea to double-check the congruence between the references cited in your article and your reference list prior to this stage, so you have time to track down any references you need to add or change. Also, if you have updated references, due to the amount of time that may have passed between when you first submitted your article and subsequent acceptance, you may add them at this time. Finally, check all URLs and update them as needed.

KARMEN'S EXPERIENCE

Arriving at her office, Karmen checks her mail. Among the junk mail, she sees a manila envelope from one of the journals to which she submitted an article. Excited and fearful, she opens the envelope to find a letter from the editor. It states that her article has not been accepted for publication, but that the reviewers have recommended that she revise and resubmit her work. Karmen immediately begins to feel dejected. So much work, so many months, and now rejection. However, as she reads the reviewers' comments along with the editor's decision, she begins to feel more relaxed. She realizes that most of the reviewers' suggestions are reasonable and would in all likelihood improve the quality of her article. She smiles to herself and begins to plot out a strategy for revising her work. She discusses the feedback with her mentor and subsequently gets her revised article back out in two weeks.

Chapter 7

COLLABORATION

In many ways, being a scholar is a lonely pursuit. We are judged on individual achievements that for the most part we perform by ourselves. Reading is a solitary act, and we are taught that writing is an equally solitary act. Many people become tired of the lonely hours of writing and avoid it. The writing of this book demanded many hours alone, cut off from friends and family. Sometimes, it hardly seems worth it.

However, although it is true that writing is often a solitary act, many of our writing projects have been done in collaboration with others. Writing collaborations can help academics break out of isolated roles and build a sense of community. We have become close to several faculty in large part because of the time we spent together during writing projects. Moore (2003) stresses the challenges and importance of collaboration: "People writing as part of a community of writers are more likely to learn faster about the conventions and challenges of writing, to support each other at times of blockages and to demystify the process of writing by sharing each others' successes and failures. This approach challenges many of the cultural and competitive conventions of academic life" (p. 334).

Collaboration also makes sense from the perspective of efficiency. When collaborating with others on articles, each person may take primary responsibility for one or more sections of the article. This helps reduce the amount of time that it takes for articles to be written. Also, when you include other faculty members on articles for which you are the primary author, they are more likely to include you on their projects.

Recently, three junior faculty and I (Rich) decided to work collaboratively on three different articles and share authorship on each. Each of us has been responsible for adding intellectual capital to each project, which justifies the inclusion of our names on each article.

Also, having three other scholars with different perspectives, training, and focus has helped enrich each article. We therefore have coauthored three articles in little more time than it would have taken to produce one or two.

Collaboration also helps push us in our work. It is harder to rationalize work expectations and schedules when we have made commitments to others. A healthy sort of peer pressure and a touch of friendly competition add well to the mix. We do not want to confuse healthy competition based on mutual collaboration and group investment, with the type of cutthroat competition that is the cultural norm in some departments. This dysfunctional competition not only is emotionally draining, but also often runs counter to rational self-interest. People who experience a sense of community with others may feel less isolated, have improved emotional health, and in general be better able to meet their psychosocial needs. Again, you will need to understand how your institution views coauthored articles before you invest too much time and energy in this process.

MENTOR–MENTEE COLLABORATION

Find a mentor that has a working style that matches your learning style. Once you find this person, be open and direct about needing help or wanting to help on his or her projects. A mentor should be a person you trust and like; it will make learning and working with him or her a pleasure and allow you to take things that will help you in your future career.

Amanda Edwards-Stewart, PhD
University of Washington Tacoma
Personal correspondence

We all need mentorship during our careers. Mentors help guide junior faculty through the many challenges they face adapting to life in academia. Mentors help us understand the political realities of institutions and the expectations within and outside of departments. Some mentors also help junior faculty learn how to be good teachers. However, one role of mentorship that is often lacking is in the area of writing and publication. Too often, mentors merely inquire about the junior faculty member's research and encourage him or her to publish.

Unfortunately, only inquiring about a new scholar's work is hardly enough. Mentors who include junior faculty on writing projects of their own provide new professors with invaluable experience. Being included on writing projects, however, should not consist of doing literature searches and copying articles. Of course, we all have to put in this type of grunt work, but doling out menial tasks to eager young PhDs only increases their burden. Even if they are included on a publication, the junior faculty members are not empowered from learning the processes and skills required to publish. Ideally, mentors should include junior faculty in all phases of the creation of an article, including initial brainstorming sessions in which new ideas are generated. Most research and scholarly articles can take many different directions. It is invaluable to learn to think through the many decisions that need to be made before an article is completed.

Berger (1990) developed a formal mentoring program in his department. His program, Getting Published, provides support to faculty interested in engaging with a mentor for the purpose of bringing articles to publication. In the first hour-long meeting, mentor and mentee discuss the types of help needed. At the end of the meeting, the mentee decides if he or she wants to engage in the program. If so, he or she submits for critique an initial manuscript that is currently being worked on. The manuscript may be the very beginnings of an idea or an article that a journal previously rejected. Berger suggests that the first manuscript worked on be one that has a high likelihood of being published as a means of achieving early success for the mentee. The mentor then evaluates the manuscript in terms of organization, clarity of conceptualization, use of literature, writing style, and grammar. Problems that occur repeatedly are identified as targets for skill improvement. The mentor then meets with the mentee in biweekly meetings. For writers who have difficulty completing their agreed-upon tasks and deadlines, short check-ins provide support, encouragement, and structure.

The help that mentors provide to writers varies on the basis of writers' individual needs, taking into account the overall goal of publishing high-quality scholarship. The program can help with many facets of the writing process, including the selection and refining of problem statements, the literature review, grammar and style issues, selection of a journal, data analysis, data presentation, and understanding of the editorial process.

> My advice is to work with a mentor you get along with, and to choose someone who has similar interests. It is helpful to work with someone who has extensive knowledge of your interests as it lends itself to furthering your own knowledge base and engaging in deeper dialogue with your mentor. Most importantly, the success in any collaboration with a mentor is one based on respect and trust. If you respect your mentor, you will be more motivated in building the relationship and learning from him or her. Similarly, you need a mentor who respects you and trusts the quality of your work, even if you don't have the same degree and experience.
>
> Jennifer June, BA
> The National Center for Telehealth and Technology
> Personal correspondence

Berger (1990) asserts that it is often not enough for mentors to help faculty with the ins and outs of writing. He also believes that a motivational program is needed to help authors. This component of the program consists of five parts: (1) the work plan or timetable, (2) mentor as motivator, (3) the writing assessment interview, (4) projecting positive consequences of publishing, and (5) channeling anger.

Helping mentees work on work plans or timetables for their writing is essential. As previously noted, structure is key in the discipline of writing. In mentors' role as motivators, Berger argues that mentors should provide mentees with a great deal of positive reinforcement. This is important given the negative feelings that many of the mentees will have about writing. In the writing assessment interview, the mentor helps the mentee identify positive correlates to his or her good writing habits and barriers to such writing. The mentor also should help mentees take into account the future positive consequences of publishing. He suggests that authors be helped to visualize the pride they will feel once their article is published and recognized by peers. Mentors also help mentees understand the potential positive consequences that publishing can have on their careers. Finally, Berger argues that authors frequently harbor anger toward the publication process, as well as at the tenure and promotion processes, and they must channel anger in productive ways.

When developing scholars begin job hunting, it is important that their potential employers believe that they are competent scholars in and of themselves and have not merely ridden on the coattails of their mentors. It is for this reason that it is important that mentees be encouraged to publish scholarship on their own or with others. Although the junior scholar may desire or feel obliged to include his or her mentor as a second author on the majority of projects, it is important for mentors, at times, to discourage this practice. The mentor and mentee must discuss the reasons for this so feelings are not hurt. These are complicated issues in often-complicated relationships, with clear ethical considerations.

Much of this section applies to both mentors and mentees, though in some ways we address mentors more directly, as it is their responsibility to provide good mentorship. It is one of the key ways that, as mentors, we can give back to our professions. However, this does not mean that developing scholars and practitioners hoping to publish are free of responsibility. There is much to gain from good mentorship. Sadly, though, good mentorship is not always easy to find. By being clear about your abilities and needs, you can help your mentor better serve you as a scholar. At times you will need to be proactive, as senior scholars have many demands on their time. However, by discussing the nature of your collaborative relationship, you will be able to negotiate with your mentor around any difficulties that may arise.

THE WRITING CIRCLE OR GROUP

Writing groups can be a wonderful way of establishing connections with others who have the same ultimate goal of publishing articles. Several models exist for writing-group collaborations. One model that works well is for each member of the group to pick an article on which he or she will include others as secondary authors. This works best with small groups of four or five people. When you form a writing group, discuss what processes and procedures each of you finds helpful. You may even wish to use this book as a guide and go over each chapter as a way of mastering new skills.

Page-Adams, Cheng, Gogineni, and Shen (1995) established a student writing group of eight of the twenty-five doctoral students enrolled in a program at Washington University. The goal of this group was to encourage doctoral students to write for publication by providing them with support, setting deadlines for drafts, and giving them regular in-depth critiques of their work. The group procured the support of the school's administration for a meeting space and copying privileges. Page-Adams and colleagues (1995) view this institutional support as key to the program's success.

During the meetings, the students provide one another with feedback on three main areas: conceptualization, substantive content, and writing style. In the early sessions, they also discussed whether an article was worth writing in terms of its potential to make a scholarly contribution and thus to be publishable. The group members found that they had several common weaknesses to their work, including inadequate descriptions of relevant theoretical traditions, poorly detailed assumptions, and insufficient considerations of the implications of the work for theory, research, or practice. They learned that by normalizing the revisions process they were able to commit to the difficult work of writing without becoming demoralized.

The authors conducted an evaluation of the group by comparing the number of articles members of the group completed and submitted for publication to those completed and submitted by a similar group of their peers (Page-Adams et al., 1995). The results indicated that participation in the writing group helped doctoral students produce more scholarship than peers who did not participate, as well as more scholarship than previous participants.

A potential challenge of the peer writing group is embarrassment. Perhaps because many doctoral programs do not provide instruction on scholarly writing (Murray & MacKay, 1998), many academics may feel uncertain about their writing skills. Certainly, we all have room to grow (refer to chapter 2 to help increase insight into your strengths and limitations as a writer). However, it is important to recognize that you do have the abilities required to complete your work.

Clance and Imes (1978) coined the phrase "imposter syndrome." This is not a true psychological diagnosis, but rather a description of an experience common to many high achievers. Essentially, the individual feels that he or she has gained current status (such as admittance into a graduate program or gaining a tenure-track faculty position) by accident or mistake. The individual tends to feel that he or she is not truly qualified to perform adequately and that he or she will be discovered at any time (Beck, 2010). Keep in mind that your peers may feel similarly embarrassed. By showing your work to them, you are actually giving them a great gift: you are inviting them to show their work to you.

Waiting until your writing seems perfect to show it to others is a poor strategy. If you are already anxious about your writing abilities, it is unlikely that you will get your work to the state that you desire, and you may find yourself saying, "just one more revision" multiple times. Also, it is simply inefficient. A peer writer can quickly confirm what is working and what is not. Try to get feedback from a peer in your discipline and a peer unfamiliar with your topic area. The former can help identify areas that need more depth and the latter can help identify spots that need more clarity.

Writing groups can be quite informal. A few of my coworkers have five minutes set aside on their schedule each month when they gather around the water cooler to state their progress during the previous month and their goals for the next. For these individuals, simply stating goals out loud and knowing that they will need to report back to the group at a specific time provides the motivation they need to stay on track with their writing production goals.

ISSUES OF AUTHORSHIP

When you decide to include others as secondary authors, it is important to include them in real, meaningful ways. Merely editing a document does not warrant authorship. However, when someone lends intellectual capital to your work, such as contributing to or formulating literature reviews, helping conceptualize important findings, and helping write conclusions that have relevance to your profession, you should offer that colleague authorship. In fact, many professions have codes of ethics that mandate that contributions such as these be recognized in authorship. Frequently, students and junior faculty do not receive credit for ideas or work that they contributed, or they receive second authorship solely because of the status of one of the contributors. It is difficult to contend with this situation, as senior scholars certainly hold significant power within their departments and professions. Young scholars and graduate students may be concerned that if they assert their right to authorship, then they will be rejected by the senior scholar. Such political decisions that affect one's personal future should not be minimized. Before asserting authorship demands, it is important to balance what is right and just, with what is wise.

Chapter 8

ETHICS, PITFALLS, AND PROBLEMS

Ethical issues hold a central place in scholarship and publication (Erlen, 2002). Without a proper understanding of ethical considerations, graduate students, scholars, and practitioners put their present and future careers at risk. This section will explore the various ethical issues that cut across disciplinary boundaries and are common to most, if not all, publications. It is important to note that you must consult several sources when considering ethical issues. First, make certain you know your professional society's ethical positions concerning publishing. Second, contributors' guides or notes to authors often contain important information regarding the expectations of the journal. Submitting an article to a specific publication signifies that you are in agreement with their guidelines.

ORIGINALITY OF IDEAS AND PLAGIARISM

Although it seems that scholars and practitioners would not need to be reminded of the perils of plagiarism, it is an important ethical concern that every writer must keep in mind. With the advent and proliferation of electronic sources and the Internet, information has become increasingly easy to obtain. In many ways, it has become increasingly easy to be careless with ascribing credit for the ideas you have obtained. However inadvertent, failing to give credit through cited quotations or at least citation constitutes plagiarism and is an ethical violation.

ETHICS IN RESEARCH

It is important that long before you submit your article for publication, you carefully consider the ethical ramifications of your research. Since many researchers in the human services seek to conduct research with vulnerable populations, processes have been put in place to help researchers ensure the well-being of their participants. All universities have an institutional review board (IRB) that helps faculty understand the ethical dimensions of their research. Many large agencies also have IRBs or arrange to use the services of IRBs from other institutions (e.g., large agencies, universities, hospitals). It is essential that you present any research involving human subjects to the appropriate IRB in order to protect you, potential research participants, and your institution. In some institutions, research that is not conducted on live human beings (i.e., policy research using archived data) is fully exempt from IRB consideration. At other institutions, researchers must fill out some paperwork and allow the IRB to decide whether research is exempt from full review. Regardless, it is essential that you know the IRB and human subjects protocols at your university or agency, or both.

In addition, it is important that you consider the ethical implications of your chosen area of research and your methodology. One good strategy is to read research that is similar in terms of both subject matter and methods and to consider how those researchers have grappled with ethical concerns.

SIMULTANEOUS SUBMISSIONS

It is important to understand the taboo of simultaneous submissions. An article can only be submitted to one journal at a time. Even if a journal does not explicitly address simultaneous submissions in their guidelines, this is considered standard practice and must be followed in all cases. While it is frustrating to have to wait months for an article to make it through the review process before finding out if it will be accepted or rejected, it is essential that you submit a particular article to only one journal at a time. Editors and review board members usually are not paid staff members, but rather are professionals and academics. They provide a valuable service to the profession and to authors who submit their work. To submit an article without the intention of publishing it in a given journal wastes their valuable time.

Complexities do occur from time to time. I (Rich) once submitted an article for publication to a journal that, unknown to me at the time, was going through a bit of turmoil and confusion. After several months, I wrote the editor to whom I submitted my work and got no response. A month went by and still I heard nothing, so I both wrote and called. After another month or two had passed, I left a message on the editor's telephone that I was going to withdraw the article and submit it to another journal (this step should have included a written letter, and I should have kept a copy of it for my own protection). The following day, I submitted the article to another journal. In about two weeks, the editor of the first journal emailed with an apologetic note and an acceptance of my article. This put me in a bind. I had resubmitted the article to another journal and had already received a letter that my article was in that journal's review process. Yet this situation occurred very early in my career, and it was difficult to imagine giving up a certain publication. After consultation with two senior faculty, I wrote a letter to the second journal withdrawing my article from consideration. In the letter, I carefully explained the situation and my awareness of the ethical implications of simultaneous submissions, and I clearly apologized for the unfortunate situation. Fortunately, the editor understood.

One of the key lessons for me here was to seek guidance from my mentors and supervisors. It was important to seek their guidance and keep them abreast of any potential circumstances in which my ethical judgment could be questioned. Another potential source of consultation is professional associations. Most have at least one officer or attorney whose job is to help members interpret ethical guidelines and develop appropriate responses.

ETHICS OF AUTHORSHIP

We have touched on authorship previously in this chapter; it is an important consideration in the publication process. Authorship is meant to signify a meaningful contribution and approval of the work. It is not a reward, gift, or honorarium, but signifies intensive and meaningful intellectual work. Authorship should be assigned to those who engage in the conceptualization of the research design of the project, the intellectual formulation of the article, or the actual writing of the document (APA, 2009). It is not assigned to someone who simply has made editorial corrections.

ETHICAL OBLIGATIONS OF
MENTORS AND SENIOR SCHOLARS

The ethics-of-care perspective is different from many systems of ethics in that it views the context between parties as an important factor in making ethical decisions (Rhodes, 1985). Unlike rights-based systems of ethics in which a particular action is right or wrong regardless of the situation, the ethics-of-care perspective asserts that one cannot separate issues of right and wrong from one's obligations from his or her relationships and responsibilities to others. According to Beauchamp and Childress (1994, p. 246), ethics of care places emphasis on "traits valued in intimate, personal relationships [including] sympathy, compassion, fidelity, discernment and love. Caring in these accounts refers to care for, emotional commitment to, and willingness to act on the behavior of persons with whom one has a significant relationship" (p. 85).

It is important that mentors take care to understand the nature of their ethical obligations toward their mentees. The role of the mentor vis-à-vis scholarship is not only to help mentees publish, but also to help them develop skills that will encourage development of scholarly excellence. Further, while it is valuable to include mentees on projects and mentors certainly feel grateful when mentees reciprocate by including them, it is important that mentors look out for their mentees' long-term interests. It is important that mentees be encouraged to work on projects with other people as well as to work independently, so others do not perceive that they have been riding on the mentor's coattails. In the mentor–mentee relationship, mentors are ethically responsible for being clear in their communication, for helping the mentee understand the nature of the relationship, and for being willing to discuss issues that mentees may feel hesitant to bring up if they feel indebted to their mentor. Mentors must make sure that they are aware of their power and influence and that they never take advantage of their mentees' relatively vulnerable positions. Many graduate schools have guidelines that address the mentor–mentee relationship; if you are not affiliated with an institution that has one, we suggest you develop such a document for any mentor–mentee relationship you enter into. The document should clearly spell out the nature of the relationship and discuss issues such as authorship and the use of mentors' time.

JOURNALS' OBLIGATIONS TO AUTHORS

Whereas the focus of this chapter has been on the ethical responsibilities of authors of scholarship, journal editorial staff also have obligations toward their authors and potential authors. Since many beginning scholars will become editors, editorial board members, or reviewers themselves, if they are not already, these obligations may be of help to all readers. First, it is important to remember that in a very real sense people's lives, or at least their livelihoods, are affected by the decisions and actions of editors and review board members. While this certainly does not mean that authors have an entitlement to publication, they should be entitled to fair and ethical treatment.

Perhaps the most difficult issue to contend with is review times. Some journals give guidelines for how long their reviews take, but others do not. It is important for editors to take their review guidelines seriously and revise them when they are unrealistic. If a journal states that its reviews take three to four months to complete, yet reviews rarely occur within this time frame, it is important that editors change their guidelines to correspond with the actual review times and communicate this clearly to potential authors. Editors have an ethical responsibility to make sure that articles are reviewed in a timely fashion. Late reviews place editors in difficult administrative and ethical dilemmas, as they are dependent on reviewers and their timeliness in providing feedback. Reviewers also have ethical responsibilities toward authors for providing timely reviews. In order to avoid problems, editors would do well to enumerate their expectations to reviewers in clear and direct guidelines. It is reasonable for reviewers to frame the importance of following review guidelines in terms of ethical obligations toward one's colleagues and one's profession. Clearly, such guidelines must be presented in a collegial manner. Framing such issues in terms of ethical obligations can help reviewers see the importance of their role. Be certain, however, that when you engage editors about these issues you are constructive and not attacking.

KARMEN CONFRONTS THE ETHICS OF AUTHORSHIP

Karmen together with two of her colleagues submitted an article. She was the third author of the article and did not believe she had contributed as much as she normally would have. In fact, the second author took out some of her contribution, leaving her contribution in question in her mind. However, the first author assured her that her contribution was sufficient to warrant authorship. When the article came back from review, the first author shared the feedback with her. One of the comments had to do with a concern about informed consent of the research participants. In discussing the revisions, the second author, who had procured the data, agreed to address the issue. During email discussions about the revisions, it was decided that Karmen would do further analysis, of the type she originally had contributed. The first author suggested that Karmen do her analysis while the second author worked on his response to the concerns about client protection. Karmen agreed, but upon reflection she again became uncomfortable. She agreed with the reviewers' concerns and wanted to be certain her name would not appear on an article with questionable research ethics. Additionally, she did not want to commit her time and effort to the project before she could be certain that these issues could be resolved. Karmen was able to bring her concerns to the attention of the first author, who agreed that the ethical issues should be resolved before she committed additional work on the article.

PITFALLS

It would be wonderful if others always treated us kindly, well, with respect, and in accordance to good social graces. However, the universe does not always behave the way we wish it would, and it is no different when it comes to publishing. In this section, we present several of the most common pitfalls when it comes to the publication process, and attempt to explore potential solutions. However, each human encounter is different, and you will be called on to exercise your judgment and discretion in complex situations. One word of advice: proceed slowly when problems occur. Seek the advice of trusted colleagues who have experience with publication or at least the advice of trusted confidants who understand the needs and demands of your work and profession.

Nonresponsive or Difficult Editors

As we have stated, the role of editor is often thankless and stressful. Most editors do their work exceptionally well and provide a great service to potential authors. They are often some of our best allies in our development as scholars. However, editors are human beings, and with human beings come variance and a wealth of behaviors and motivations that are sometimes less than desirable.

A common problem is the nonresponsive editor. Editorial nonresponsiveness can occur during many phases and can be particularly frustrating once an article is well into the review process. One key is to identify the problem early on. In the sample submission letter (appendix D) and revision letters (appendixes E and F), you will note that we ask editors to contact us via email or traditional mail to confirm the receipt of our work. The vast majority of editors will do this as a matter of policy, and usually within the first several weeks. However, we like to have it in our cover letter just to establish contact and to ensure that we will know that our work has been received. If we do not hear back, we contact the editor via email within a month. If we do not hear back within another several days, we attempt to call. After this, we send another email and then phone within another week.

If you follow these steps and continue to get no response, you have two options. First, contact the publisher; the leadership of the journal or the editor's contact information may have changed. However, if you do indeed have the correct information, this alerts the publisher that the journal may not be attended to in the most helpful manner. You deserve contact.

If the editor responds at this point, you must determine how dedicated and helpful the editor will be. If the process has already taken nearly two months, how long might your article spend in review? It is fair to ask this question in the most polite and gentle yet firm, hostility-free manner. If you are not completely satisfied, and it is not a journal that you feel you absolutely must publish in, I suggest cutting your losses and submitting your work elsewhere. Should you choose to do this, you must inform the original editor of this decision. As it would be an ethical breach to submit the same article simultaneously to two journals, be sure to save a copy of your letter (which you should send via registered mail, if possible).

Sometimes, though rarely, editors may be less than pleasant. This is one argument for sending a query letter, as it allows you to see how well the editor may respond to you. However, some difficulties are only identified later in the process. It is important that in such situations you maintain a professional attitude and do not engage the editor in a confrontation. I (Rich) once made the mistake of allowing myself to get into a negative email exchange with an editor who decided that I must not have paid close attention to the scope and range of his journal, since my article was totally inappropriate. As I had queried, had carefully read the guidelines for the journal, and had read through the tables of contents of several volumes, I thought my article was appropriate. Had either of us complained to the other's supervisors, I am sure it would not have looked very good. Yet he was a full professor and I was a very new assistant professor—not a wise battle for me to have engaged in.

Difficulties with Collaborators

Even though I have strongly advocated collaborating with others, collaboration is not without its potential pitfalls. When you are working with collaborators, prevention is important. You must choose your collaborators well and attempt graciously to avoid working with those you do not believe will hold up their end of the bargain. During the early stages of your work together, set clear guidelines in terms of roles and responsibilities and make sure to develop a time line. Be prepared to be flexible and understanding. Having a colleague miss a deadline by a week is not a tragedy. Be as supportive to others as you would want them to be with you. However, if a great deal of time has passed, or your colleague has repeatedly failed to live up to your agreements, you may have to renegotiate the work arrangement. Again, it is important to think about the nature of your relationship and your need for the work to be sent out quickly. I attempt to have several projects going at any given time, and allow for several to develop more slowly. This type of flexibility allows me to work with those whose adherence to deadlines may not be as rigid as my own.

At times, you will find that even though you have thought carefully about with whom you wish to collaborate, you learn that you and your colleague work too differently. In your own mind, you may attribute your challenges to problems or deficits that you perceive in your colleague. True or not, it is best to attempt to view such struggles as a sign of differences that may or may not be reconcilable. It is best to approach your colleague about these terms and explore ways you can negotiate around your stylistic and scholarly differences. If either of you perceives that you cannot overcome these obstacles alone, you may wish to include another colleague as an impartial mediator. If not, it is good to thank your collaborator for his or her effort and negotiate the process of separating your work. Again, should this prove difficult, you may want to involve an impartial mediator in the process.

Shifting and Changing Tenure Guidelines

For academics, the tenure and promotion process is one of the most stressful aspects of our job. Before tenure, junior faculty attempt to align their work production to the expectations of multiple constituents, including students, department colleagues, university colleagues, family, and self. Each of these players has a potentially different view of what a young scholar's work life should be like. Achieving a balance is never easy.

Another difficulty is that tenure and promotion guidelines are not always static. Although such guidelines are in writing, they are often open to interpretation and may be subject to change. While junior faculty are supposed to be evaluated under the tenure guidelines with which they were hired, this is often not the case. Therefore, it is important to understand the political and cultural climate of your institution, as well as the vision of its leaders. For instance, if your university is in the process of becoming a research institution, expectations for what this means may be unrealistic in terms of the amount of support available. Knowing the dynamics of your university or department up front can help you understand how expectations may change. As a rule of thumb, in most professional disciplines publishing several first authored articles in good peer-reviewed, indexed journals is one of the best ways to inoculate yourself against shifting expectations. Book chapters and books themselves go in and out of acceptance in certain institutions, but refereed journal articles tend to remain central to most human services disciplines.

Your Own Style and Behavior

As we have previously discussed, we each bring our own personal strengths and limitations to the writing and publishing process. At times, our own personal style and behavior can be what gets in our way during many phases of the process. For instance, those who have a hard time being patient may have a difficult time waiting through a slow editorial process. In such situations, it is important that you work to keep your annoyance in check before you contact an editor. Others have a hard time with insecurity and feel devastated when an article comes back rejected. As with life in general, we each need to learn how to compensate for our weaknesses and to know ourselves well enough to understand when the best course of action is inaction. We encourage you to use your academic notebook as a means to help process the difficult feelings and issues that come up during the process.

Chapter 9

CONCLUSION

In this brief closing chapter, we present steps for continued professional development and some final thoughts on the process of developing as a scholar.

READ JOURNALS

While it may seem obvious, becoming a good reader is one of the best ways to become a good writer. This may be particularly true of journal articles, as they have a specialized format and structure. A good rule of thumb is to frequently read the journals in which you want to publish and the core journals in your profession. It is important to read various types of journals as a means of expanding your knowledge and learning new approaches to problems. To develop novel approaches to problems, it is helpful to read the work of those who are thinking and writing in new and creative ways. Periodically reading outside your discipline helps avoid overly confined thinking.

BECOME A REVIEWER

Becoming a reviewer is one of the best ways to improve your skills as a writer for publication. It also gives you firsthand insights into the inner workings of the review process and allows you to understand what authors do that is effective and what they do that does not work. Try to become a reviewer early on in your career, but make certain you do not agree to review too many articles, which can be time consuming.

BECOME AN EDITORIAL BOARD MEMBER

Becoming an editorial board member helps you understand how journals work and how decision making occurs in the publication process.

It helps you make contacts with others in the field and is a sign of your development as a scholar.

BECOME AN EDITOR

Not a responsibility to take lightly, being an editor is an extremely time-consuming and often thankless job. Being the editor of a journal is often an unpaid position. If you are thinking about becoming an editor of a journal, it is important that your institution provide you with work release to complete your tasks.

WORK ON VARIOUS TYPES OF ARTICLES

Try to work on projects that take you out of your comfort zone. If you are a quantitative researcher, for example, try to work on a theoretical article. If you tend to do policy work, try to do an autoethnographic study. Pushing the boundaries of what you are comfortable with will help you develop as a scholar and will prevent you from feeling burned out or stale.

COLLABORATE WITH NEW PEOPLE, DIFFERENT DISCIPLINES

Collaborating with new people can bring the energy we need to our work. Different disciplines approach problems from different vantage points. Working with new colleagues from disciplines different from your own is valuable for several reasons. First, we must be very clear about our own work and concepts so that we are able to explain them to colleagues who have a different vocabulary from our own. We will discover quickly when working with those trained in other fields which of our ideas are fuzzy or vague and which are clear. Second, working with colleagues from other disciplines allows you to expand your own knowledge by connecting it to other ideas. You may find it incredibly stimulating to listen to how new colleagues approach issues and problems. Finally, interdisciplinary work often brings a richness to our scholarship that is lacking when our work becomes insular and even parochial.

We hope this book has provided you with some guidelines that will help you get your work published. It is our hope that you have also begun to consciously think about what is possible to do as a scholar and who you want to become. While publishing is a worthwhile goal, and certainly one with important benefits, what is really important is the journey of developing as scholars and, indeed, as human beings.

Appendix A

WRITING RESOURCES

Internet Sites

http://www.dictionary.com
A website that provides useful writing tools such as a thesaurus and guidelines for grammatical uses.

http://www.bartleby.com
A good source of reference material that is free of charge.

http://writing-program.uchicago.edu/resources/grammar.htm
A useful website of grammar resources from the University of Chicago Writing Program that is especially good for learning and understanding grammatical rules. It includes a model for understanding grammar.

Books and Articles

American Psychological Association (APA). (2009). *Publication manual of the American Psychological Association* (6th ed., 2nd printing). Washington, DC: Author.

Baretta-Herman, A. L., & Garrett, K. J. (2000). Faculty-student collaboration: Issues and recommendations. *Advances in Social Work, 1,* 148–159.

Becker, H. S. (1998). *Tricks of the trade: How to think about your research while you're doing it.* Chicago: University of Chicago Press.

Carroll-Johnson, R. M. (2001). Submitting a manuscript for review. *Clinical Journal of Oncology Nursing, 5,* 13–16.

Drisko, J. (1999). Reviewing a manuscript: The reviewer's experience and standards. *Families in Society, 80,* 417–419.

Gibelman & Gelman. (1999). "Who's the author?": Ethical issues in publishing. *Aretê, 23,* 77–88.

Gobel, B. H. (2001). Getting started. *Clinical Journal of Oncology Nursing, 5,* 3-6.

Gray, M. (1999). Writing for a journal: Blood, sweat, and tears. *Families in Society, 80,* 305-307.

King, C. R. (2001). Ethical issues in writing and publishing. *Clinical Journal of Oncology Nursing, 5,* 19-23.

Kirk, S. (1993). The puzzles of peer perusal. *Social Work Research & Abstracts, 29,* 3-4.

Mee, C. L. (2001). 10 Lessons on writing for publication. *Clinical Journal of Oncology Nursing, 5,* 25-26.

Netting, F. E., & Nichols-Casebolt, A. (1997). Authorship and collaboration: Preparing the next generation of social work scholars. *Journal of Social Work Education, 33,* 555-564.

Pan, M. L. (2008). *Preparing literature reviews: Qualitative and quantitative approaches* (3rd ed.). Glendale, CA: Pyrczak Publishing.

Pyrczak, F., & Bruce, R. R. (2007). *Writing empirical research reports: A basic guide for students of the social and behavioral sciences* (6th ed.). Glendale, CA: Pyrczak Publishing.

Reibschleger, J. (2001). Writing a dissertation: Lessons learned. *Families in Society, 82,* 579-582.

Sigler, B. (2001). Signing on the dotted line. *Clinical Journal of Oncology Nursing, 5,* 17-18.

Simpson, R. (1990). The ethical responsibilities of referees. *American Sociologist, 21,* 80-83.

Swales, J. M., & Feak, C. B. (2000). Unit 4: The literature review (pp. 114-147). Unit 5: More complex literature reviews (pp. 148-186). In *English in today's research world: A writing guide.* Ann Arbor: University of Michigan Press.

Tasker, M. (1999). "Tell me about it": The agony and ecstasy of writing for publication. *Families in Society, 80,* 649-651.

Thyer, B. A. (2008). *Preparing research articles.* New York: Oxford University Press.

University of Chicago. (2010). *Chicago manual of style* (16th ed.). Chicago: Author.

Zinsser, W. (1998). *Writing to learn.* New York: Harper & Row.

Appendix B

SOURCES FOR
LOCATING JOURNALS

http://www.doaj.org

The Directory of Open-Access Journals contains detailed information and links to more than 1,800 journals. The database is searchable by title or subject and allows searches of more than 400 journals by article name, making it excellent for research as well.

http://www.psycline.org/

Far more than a database of psychology journals, Psycline includes descriptions of and links to more than 2,000 journals from across the human services and helping professions. Links are provided to both traditional print journals and electronic sources. The database allows for searches by keyword, subject, and journal type.

http://www.eric.ed.gov

ERIC (Education Resources Information Center) is a digital library of educational materials sponsored by the U.S. Department of Education. It provides the comprehensive source of journals related to education, and basic information about hundreds of journals. Although ERIC does not provide links to the journals, perusing the titles can be of value when you are looking for potential publication sources. If your institution has a subscription to ERIC, you will be able to obtain full-text materials online.

http://ergo.asu.edu/ejdirectory.html

The American Educational Research Association Special Interest Group is a wonderful list of open-access journals related to teaching and education from around the world. In addition to being a good source of potential venues for publication, it is a way of finding information regarding teaching, pedagogy, and education.

http://www.nursingcenter.com/library/index.asp

Nursing Center.com provides various valuable resources for nursing and nursing students and lists more than fifty journals applicable to nurses.

Appendix C

SAMPLE LETTER TO THE EDITOR

IN RESPONSE TO POINT/COUNTERPOINT "THE ROLE OF THEORY IN RESEARCH ON SOCIAL WORK PRACTICE," BY BRUCE A. THYER & TOMI GOMORY, *JOURNAL OF SOCIAL WORK EDUCATION* (WINTER 2001).

To the editor:

The Point/Counterpoint "The Role of Theory in Research on Social Work Practice" (Winter 2001) struck me as an ironic and tragic example of the irrelevance of much social work scholarship to social work practitioners and educators alike. For nearly eighty pages, the authors theorize about the relevance of theory. Both authors present erudite and effective arguments to support their points that could have been made in a few pages. This excess is not the fault of the authors: it is the editorial staff's responsibility to shape the structure and length of such debates.

Dr. Thyer argues that there is a crisis among and between social work scholars and practitioners. He cogently argues that the crisis pertains to the overrepresentation of theoretical scholarship in an applied discipline. He insists that studies pertaining to the effectiveness of social programs and intervention should be our primary focus. While I agree such research is very important, I disagree that this represents a crisis. That there is a crisis I wholeheartedly agree.

In fact, the very debate between these two fine scholars is indicative of the crisis. The true crisis in scholarship within social work and social work education is over the relevance and accessibility of the productions of scholarship (journal articles) to the practitioners they are meant to inform. Whether that practitioner is a social work educator or line-level practitioner, a reader must be able to find some connection between his or her day-to-day work experiences and what is written. Writing must be interesting, lively, and real. Writing that educates is that which comes alive and dances on the interface of practice and thought. Erudite as the authors of the articles in question may be, the debate in question will not be of great interest to very many social work faculty.

Many of our journals are full of dry, overly intellectualized works that put us to sleep. Who needs Ambien or Trazadone when a good journal is nearby? Practice wisdom that practitioners can connect with and learn from is rare. Advice and guidance for educators whose most important role is the actual training of the social workers of tomorrow is noticeably absent.

Why are we so afraid to be clear, simple, and relevant? Dr. Thyer was correct in asserting that we are still enormously impacted by Flexner's now ancient critique of our knowledge base. For nearly a century, many faculty within social work education have reacted to this attack by adopting postures of pseudo science and pseudo intellectualism. Frankly, we want people to think we are smart. We pander to the academy and forget our roots.

How does this affect our relationships to our students? How does it impact our relationships to oppressed people (assuming most of us still have contact)? More significantly, how does this affect our ability to teach and inform each other? Frankly, I am tired of such mental gymnastics.

Where are writers who teach real, down-to-earth practice wisdom, like Donald Krill, or the late Howard Goldstein?

Come down to earth and play with us little people. We won't bite. I would encourage the editors to think about the daily activities and needs of social work educators. Perhaps they could invite an empirical study of the perceptions of social work faculty regarding their needs for consumption of scholarship. This would be a courageous step towards making the journal more relevant.

Appendix D

SAMPLE SUBMISSION LETTER

September 16, 2004

Dear Dr. Smith:

Enclosed are copies of my article "Autoethnographic Poems and Narrative Reflections: A Qualitative Study of the Death of a Companion Animal" for possible publication in the *Journal of Family Social Work*. Only one of the copies has a cover page with identifying information, while the other copies start with the abstract and title.

I believe that your journal would be an excellent fit for my work. I welcome feedback regarding my scholarship and see the development of a manuscript as a collaborative process among author, editors, and reviewers. Please contact me via email if you need any additional information. I would be grateful if you could confirm that you have received my package.

Sincerely,

Rich Furman, MSW, PhD

Appendix E

SAMPLE REVISION LETTER 1

November 10, 2005

Dr. Daley:

Thank you for your letter and for providing us with the reviewers' feedback regarding our manuscript, number 05-0118, "Faculty Perceptions of Curricular Deficits in Preparing Students for Practice with Latinos." We were thrilled that you and the reviewer were so positive about the quality of our work. We were also grateful for the requested changes that we feel helped improve the article a great deal. Below I address the changes that we made. Should you deem further changes necessary, we will be glad to make them.

(1) The reviewer was surprised that this study was the first of its kind. After several extensive literature reviews, I can assure her/him it is unique.

(2) We changed the manner in which we discussed our sample, taking out claims of representativeness. We also took out references to a sampling method that was not used (our backup). We used the suggested wording of the reviewer.

(3) We also took out the reference to the appendix, which clearly was not necessary.

(4) We changed the language that was perceived as devaluing qualitative research. We are glad the reviewer caught this.

(5) We clarified the nature of the questionnaire, and the methodology in general.

(6) We created two sections where findings are presented, instead of one.

(7) We took out editorializing comments that could be viewed as privileging work with Latinos over practice with African Americans. Not our intent at all.

(8) We choose not to use bullet points for discussion points. I hope that this style preference is okay.

Thanks for your time and work on helping bring our article to press. We are truly grateful.

Sincerely,

Rich Furman, MSW, PhD

Appendix F

Sample Revision Letter 2

October 17, 2005

Re: Revisions for "An International Experience for Social Work Students: Self-Reflection through Poetry and Journal Writing Exercises"

Note: In addition to this cover page, three copies are attached without identifying information.

Dear Dr. Vigilante:

I am submitting the revisions for the above-named article for your consideration. We are grateful for the feedback of the reviewers and were heartened that there were few requested changes. Below, we explore the changes we have made, as requested by the reviewers. Of course, should you deem more changes necessary, please let me know. All revisions are placed in bold.

(1) We were pleased that one reviewer asked us to place the idea of self-reflection within a historical context. We added material from Richmond, Towle, and Hamilton. This can be found on page 5.

(2) Throughout the paper, we clarify the relationship between the exercises and self-reflection.

(3) One reviewer suggested that it is difficult to tell whether the poetry merely documents self-reflection, or whether the exercises facilitated self-reflection. While we disagree with the reviewer that this is a "laugh," we do acknowledge his/her criticism and explore this in the limitations section.

(4) We more clearly acknowledge the descriptive nature of this project in several places.
(5) In several places, we more fully acknowledge the relationship between self-reflection and practice skills.

Sincerely,

Rich Furman, MSW, PhD

REFERENCES

Alsop, C. K. (2002). Home and away: Self-reflexive auto-/ethnography. *Forum: Qualitative Social Research, 3*(3). Retrieved August 27, 2005, from http://www.qualitative-research.net/fqs-texte/3-02/3-02alsop-e.htm.

American Psychological Association (APA). (2009). *Publication manual of the American Psychological Association* (6th ed., 2nd printing). Washington, DC: APA.

Beauchamp, T. L., & Childress, J. F. (1994). *Principles of biomedical ethics*. New York: Oxford University Press.

Beck, J. S. (1995). *Cognitive therapy: Basics and beyond*. New York: Guilford Press.

Beck, J. S. (2010). Do you have the imposter syndrome? The Huffington Post. Retrieved October 7, 2010, from http://www.huffingtonpost.com/judith-s-beck-phd/the-imposter-syndrome_b_656252.html.

Berger, R. M. (1990). Getting published: A mentoring program for social work faculty. *Social Work, 35*(1), 69–71.

Blaxter, L., Hughes, C., & Tight, M. (1998). *The academic career handbook*. Philadelphia: Open University Press.

Bremer, M. (1999). *Untechnical writing*. Concord, CA: UnTechnical Press

Burns, D. D. (1999). *Feeling good: The new mood therapy* (rev. and updated). New York: Harper Collins.

Clance, P. R., & Imes, S. (1978). The imposter phenomenon in high achieving women: Dynamics and therapeutic intervention. *Psychotherapy Theory, Research and Practice, 15*(3), 1–8.

Collins, K., Furman, R., & Bruce, E. A. (2005). The use of children's literature in social work education. *Areté, 29*(2), 23–32.

Crews, K. D., & Westricnen, G. V. (2007). The "Zwolle Group" initiative for the advancement of higher education. *D-Lib Magazine, 13*(1/e). Retrieved on August 8, 2010, from http://www.dlib.org/dlib/january07/crews/01crews.html.

Doyle, E. I., Coggin, C., & Lanning, B. (2004). Writing for publication in health education. *American Journal of Health Studies, 19*(2), 100–109.

Eisner, E. W. (1991). *The enlightened eye: Qualitative inquiry and the enhancement of educational practice*. New York: Macmillan.

Ellis, A. (1958). Rational psychotherapy. *Journal of General Psychology, 59*, 37–47.

Ellis, A. (1973). My philosophy of psychotherapy. *Journal of Contemporary Psychotherapy*, 6, 13–18.

Ellis, A. (1976). *Conquering low frustration tolerance* (cassette recording). New York: Institute for Rational-Emotive Therapy.

Ellis, C., & Bouchner, A. P. (2000). Autoethnography, personal narrative, reflexivity. In N. K. Denzin & Y. S. Lincoln (Eds.), *Handbook of qualitative research* (2nd ed., pp. 733–768). Thousand Oaks, CA: Sage.

Ellis, C., & Flaherty, M. (1992). *Investigating subjectivity: Research on lived experience*. Thousand Oaks, CA: Sage.

Erlen, J. A. (2002). Writing for publication: Ethical considerations. *Orthopedic Nursing*, 12(6), 68–71.

Euben, D. R. (2002). Publish or perish: The ever-higher publication hurdle for tenure. *Academe*, July/August, 107–111.

Furman, R. (2005). Using poetry and written exercises to teach empathy. *Journal of Poetry Therapy*, 18(2), 103–110.

Furman, R., & Bender, K. (2003). The social problem of depression: A multitheoretical analysis. *Journal of Sociology and Social Welfare*, 15(3), 123–137.

Furman, R., & Jackson, R. (2002). Wrap-around services: An analysis of community-based, mental health services for children. *Journal of Child and Adolescent Psychiatric Nursing*, 15(3), 124–131.

Furman, R., Langer, C. L., & Anderson, D. K. (2006). The poet/practitioner: A new paradigm for the profession. *Journal of Sociology and Social Welfare*, 33(3), 29–50.

Furman, R., Langer, C. L., Sanchez, T. W., & Negi, N. J. (2007). A qualitative study of immigration policy and practice dilemmas for social work students. *Journal of Social Work Education*, 43(1), 133–146.

Goldstein, H. (1990). The knowledge base of social work practice: Theory, wisdom, analogue, or art? *Families and Society: The Journal of Contemporary Human Services*, 80(4), 32–41.

Greenberger, D., & Padesky, C. A. (1995). *Mind over mood: A cognitive therapy treatment manual for clients*. New York: Guilford Press.

He, Y. (2009). Strength-based mentoring in pre-service teacher education: A literature review. *Mentoring & Tutoring: Partnership in Learning*, 17(3), 263–275.

Heinrich, X., Neese, X., Rogers, X., & Facente, X. (2004). Transforming nurses into published authors. *Nursing Education Perspectives*, 25(3), 139–145.

Henson, K. T. (2005). Writing for publication: A controlled art. *Phi Delta Kappan*, June, 772–781.

Hjortshoj, K. (2001). *Understanding writing blocks*. New York: Oxford University Press.

Lanzig, J. (1997). The concept mapping homepage. Retrieved March 5, 2006, from http://users.edte.utwente.nl/lanzing/cm_home.htm.

May, R. (1979). *Psychology and the human dilemma*. New York: W.W. Norton.

Melfi, C. A., Chawla, A. J., Croghan, T. W., Hanna, M. P., Kennedy, S., & Sredl, K. (1998). The effects of adherence to antidepressant treatment guidelines on relapse and reoccurrence of depression. *Archives of General Psychiatry, 55*, 1128-1132.

Moore, S. (2003). Writers' retreats for academics: Exploring and incising the motivation to write. *Journal of Further and Higher Education, 27*(3), 333-342.

Murray, R. E. G., & MacKay, G. (1998). Supporting academic development in public output: Reflections and propositions. *International Journal for Academic Development, 3*(1), 54-63.

National Association of Social Workers (NASW). (1997). *An author's guide to social work journals* (4th ed.). Washington, DC: Author.

National Association of Social Workers (NASW). (2000). *Code of ethics of the National Association of Social Workers*. Washington, DC: Author.

Newell, R. (2000). Writing academic papers: The clinical effectiveness in nursing experience. *Clinical Effectiveness in Nursing, 4*, 93-98.

Norcross, J. C. (2005). A primer on psychotherapy integration. In J. C. Norcross & M. R. Goldfried (Eds.), *Handbook of psychotherapy integration* (pp. 3-23). New York: Oxford University Press.

Odlyzko, A. M. (1995). Tragic loss or good riddance? The impending demise of traditional scholarly journals. *International Journal of Human-Computer Studies, 42*, 71-122.

Page-Adams, D., Cheng, L. C., Gogineni, A., & Shen, C. Y. (1995). Establishing a group to encourage writing for publication among doctoral students. *Journal of Social Work Education, 31*(3), 402-407.

Parker, G., Roy, K., & Eyers, K. (2003): Cognitive behavior therapy for depression? Choose horses for courses. *American Journal of Psychiatry, 160*(5), 825-834.

Pilcher, J. J., & Walters, A. S. (1997). How sleep deprivation affects psychological variables related to college students' cognitive performance. *Journal of American College Health, 46*(3), 121-126.

Rhodes, M. L. (1985). Gilligan's theory of moral development as applied to social work. *Social Work, 30*(2), 101-105.

Richardson, L. (1993). Poetics, dramatics, and transgressive validity: The case of skipped line. *The Sociology Quarterly, 34*(4), 695-710.

Richardson, L. (2000). Writing: A method of inquiry. In N. K. Denzin & Y. S. Lincoln (Eds.), *Handbook of qualitative research* (2nd ed., pp. 923-948). Thousand Oaks, CA: Sage.

Robson, M. (2008). The driver whose heart was full of sand: Leigh's story: A play therapy case study of a bereaved child. *British Journal of Guidance and Counseling, 36*(1), 71-80.

Runco, M. A., & Pritzker, S. R. (1999). *Encyclopedia of creativity*. San Diego, CA: Academic Press.

Schiele, J. H. (1991). Publication productivity of African-American social work faculty. *Journal of Social Work Education, 27*(2), 125-134.

Sellers, S. L., Perry, R., Mathiesen, S. G., & Smith, T. (2004). Evaluation of social work journal quality: Citation versus reputational approaches. *Journal of Social Work Education, 40*, 143-160.

Seo, J., & Gromala, D. (2007). Touching light: A new framework for immersion in artistic environments. *Technoetic Arts: A Journal of Speculative Research, 5*(1), 3-14.

Shiffman, S., Paty, J. A., Gnys, M., Kassel, J. A., & Hickcox, M. (1996). First lapses to smoking: Within-subjects analysis of real-time reports. *Journal of Consulting and Clinical Psychology, 64*(2), 366-379.

Smith, S. M., & Blankenship, S. E. (1991). Incubation and the persistence of fixation in problem solving. *The American Journal of Psychology, 104*(1), 61-87.

Spry, T. (2010). Call it swing: A jazz blues autoethnography. *Cultural Studies/Critical Methodologies, 10*(4), 271-282.

Stein, H. F. (2004). A window to the interior of experience. *Families, Systems, & Health, 22*(2), 178-179.

Teggart, T. (2009). Review of *By their own young hand*: Deliberate self-harm and suicidal ideation in adolescents. *Child Care in Practice, 15*(2), 161-162.

Thyer, B. A., & Myers, L. L. (2003). An empirical evaluation of the editorial practices of social work journals. *Journal of Social Work Education, 39*, 125-140.

University of Chicago. (2010). *The Chicago manual of style* (16th ed.). Chicago: Author.

Wright, J. H., Beck, A. T., & Thase, M. E. (2008). Cognitive therapy. In R. F. Hales, S. C. Yudofsky, & G. O. Gabbard (Eds.), *The American psychiatric publishing textbook of clinical psychiatry* (5th ed.). Washington, DC: American Psychiatric Publishing.

INDEX

ABOUT THE AUTHORS

Rich Furman (MSW, University of Pennsylvania; PhD, Yeshiva University) is professor of Social Work at the University of Washington, Tacoma. He is the 2011 recipient of the University of Washington Tacoma distinguished research award. Rich has published more than one hundred scholarly articles, books, and book chapters. His most recent books are *Social Work Practice with Men at Risk, Transnational Social Work Practice, Social Work Practice with Latinos: Key Issues and Emerging Themes, An Experiential Approach to Groupwork*, and *Navigating Human Service Organizations*. Rich's main areas of research are social work practice with transnational Latino populations, men at risk and masculinities, and the use of the arts and humanities in social work practice, research, and education.

Julie T. Kinn (MA, University of North Carolina, Charlotte; PhD, University of Illinois, Chicago) is a clinical and research psychologist at the U.S. Department of Defense's National Center for Telehealth & Technology. She specializes in military suicide prevention and surveillance. She lives in Olympia, Washington, with her husband and two children.